Diagnostic Assessment

Levels 4–6

A Division of The McGraw-Hill Companies

Columbus, Ohio

www.sra4kids.com

SRA/McGraw-Hill

*A Division of The **McGraw·Hill** Companies*

Send all inquiries to:
SRA/McGraw-Hill
8787 Orion Place
Columbus, OH 43240-4027

Printed in the United States of America.

ISBN 0-07-571214-8

3 4 5 6 7 8 9 DBH 07 06 05 04

Table of Contents

Introduction . . . . v–xiii

Oral Word Reading
Introduction 2–4

Oral Fluency Introduction 5–8

Student Record and
Assessment Summary 9–11

Literacy Interview 14–16

Fourth Grade

Oral Word Reading 18–24

Oral Fluency Assessment 25–30

Spelling
Directions 32
Spelling the /er/ Sound 33–34
Short Vowels 35–36
Regular and Irregular
Plurals 37–38
Final -le, -el, -al, -il, or -ol 39–40
Long-Vowel Spelling Patterns 41–42
Frequently Misspelled Words 43–44

Vocabulary
Directions 46
Homophones 47–48
Content-Area Words 49–50
Prefixes, Suffixes, and
Root Words 51–52
Compound Words 53–54
Synonyms and Antonyms 55–56
Multiple-Meaning Words 57–58

Silent Reading Comprehension
Directions 60
Plot, Character, Conflict,
and Setting 61–62
Sequence 63–64
Cause and Effect 65–66
Author's Purpose 67–68
Persuasive Writing 69–70
Describe a Process 71–72

Fifth Grade

Oral Word Reading 73–80

Oral Fluency Assessment 81–86

Spelling
Directions 88
Different Spellings for
the /er/ Sound 89–90
Consonant Before -le
Spelling Pattern 91–92
Frequently Misspelled Words 93–94
Consonant Blends
and Digraphs 95–96
Homophones 97–98
Long-Vowel Spellings 99–100

Vocabulary
Directions 102
Word Families 103–104
Content-Area Words 105–106
Regular and Irregular
Plurals 107–108
Words with Multiple
Meanings 109–110
Compound Words 111–112
Synonyms and Antonyms 113–114

Silent Reading Comprehension
Directions 116
Plot 117–118
Making Inferences 119–120
Main Idea and Details 121–122
Cause and Effect 123–124
Sequence 125–126
Analyzing Character Traits 127–128

Sixth Grade

Oral Word Reading. 130–136

Oral Fluency Assessment 137–142

Spelling

    Directions 144

    Long-Vowel Spellings 145–146

    The /er/ Sound 147–148

    Short-Vowel Spellings. 149–150

    Homophones. 151–152

    Syllables 153–154

Vocabulary

    Directions 156

    Denotation and

       Connotation 157–158

    Compound Words 159–160

    Multiple-Meaning Words 161–162

    Word Families 163–164

    Synonyms and Antonyms. 165–166

    Understanding Idioms 167–168

    Analogies 169–170

Silent Reading Comprehension

    Directions 172

    Author's Purpose 173–174

    Main Idea and

       Supporting Details 175–176

    Characterization 177–178

    Setting. 179–180

    Sequence. 181–182

    Drawing Conclusions 183–184

Percentage Chart. . . . . Inside Back Cover

Introduction

Purpose

The *Open Court Reading* series includes a variety of assessment components designed to help the teacher meet the needs of a broad range of students. In certain circumstances additional student information will help the teacher make more informed instructional decisions regarding placement of a student in one of the *Open Court Reading* components. One such circumstance is the placement of a student who enters the class after the beginning of the school year. Another example is a student who, for one reason or another, is not making adequate progress as a result of typical instructional practices. A third example is making appropriate decisions to group students with similar learning needs for specific skill instruction.

The assessments contained in this guide are appropriate for these examples and other situations that you may encounter. The guide also recognizes that teachers have little time in a busy school day to conduct lengthy diagnostic or placement assessments. Therefore, the administration of the assessments and scoring procedures are relatively simple.

The Assessments

This guide contains a variety of assessments. The type of assessment varies depending on the grade level of the students. The assessment categories include:

- A Literacy Interview. The interview helps you gain an understanding of a student's reading behaviors and perception of reading.
- Oral Word Reading
- Oral Fluency Assessment
- Spelling
- Vocabulary
- Silent Reading Comprehension

Oral Word Reading and Oral Fluency Assessment have three levels of assessment: one for the beginning of the year, one for the middle of the year, and one for the end of the year. Directions and scoring procedures are provided for each assessment. Guidelines to help you evaluate each assessment are given at the beginning of each section.

Using the Assessments for Diagnosis

The key to improving the skills of students who are having difficulty reading is identifying the source of the problem. The assessments in this guide provide the information needed to identify the source of the problem. *Open Court Reading* provides materials appropriate for use with students of varying abilities:

Intervention Guide, Reteach, Challenge, and *English-Language Development Guide*

Although we recommend a variety of assessments and procedures for using them, you should adapt the recommendations to your students and their situations as you see fit. There is no substitute for the judgment and observations of an experienced teacher, and the assessments will be more effective when enhanced by a teacher's expertise.

When using the assessments, it is essential to keep in mind that you are trying to identify reading behaviors that a student has not yet mastered, as well as those that the student has already acquired. The most important areas in which to focus are:

- Decoding or fluency
- Oral or silent reading comprehension
- Vocabulary development

Determining a Student's Reading Level

Throughout this guide, we use the terms "at level," "below level," and "above level" to describe students' reading behavior. Although these terms are widely used in education, we believe it is worthwhile to discuss what they mean and how to determine a student's reading level.

In their most general sense, these terms describe how a student can read compared to other students in the same grade. In other words, they reflect national norms or reading behaviors. A student reading at level, for example, reads in a way that is typical of other students of the same age in the same grade. A student reading below level is not as accomplished as his or her peers, and a student above grade level is a better reader than comparable students.

From an instructional point of view, there is a second use of these terms, and that is to describe a student's reading ability within the same class. This relative use of the terms reflects local circumstances and helps the teacher make instructional decisions for his or her students. Students' reading behaviors may be distributed normally within the class, ranging from very poor to very good, with the typical student being average, but when compared with a national sample, the students may be reading somewhat below their peers. This discrepancy does not reflect intelligence or aptitude, it should be added, and can be overcome through diligent instruction, student effort, and family and community support.

A variety of information sources and methods are available to the teacher to determine a student's reading level. These sources and methods are described below:

- Teacher judgment is a dependable source of information regarding a student's reading ability when compared with the other students in a class. Observing students reading aloud, identifying which books students choose to read independently, and noting how long it takes students to read books are all good indications of how well a student can read compared to others in the class. Teachers should feel confident in using their own judgment to determine how well their students read.

■ Standardized achievement tests or state assessment results are available for most students. Because of testing cycles, the results of such assessments typically reflect end-of-year reading ability in the previous grade. Nonetheless, they are appropriate for estimating students' abilities—compared to a national group of their peers—during the first half of the following school year. Standardized and state test results are also useful to confirm a teacher's observations, and by sorting students according to their percentile or grade-level scores on the test, to establish the relative reading abilities of the students in a class.

■ The assessments that are part of *Open Court Reading* and other curriculum-based, informal assessments are a third source of information for the teacher. The Oral Fluency assessment, in which students read a grade-appropriate passage aloud, is one of the best ways to determine a student's reading ability. This assessment is particularly useful because it gives the teacher an opportunity to observe students reading grade-level materials.

When making judgments about a student's reading ability, it will be helpful to keep this question in mind: How well can the student read the instructional and recreational text in a given grade? Students who are at grade level should be able to read such texts comfortably, with minimal assistance and good comprehension. They can recall highlights of the text and can answer both literal and inferential questions about the text with an accuracy rate of between seventy and ninety percent.

Students who are reading above grade level will have an easy time reading the text, they will comprehend it thoroughly, and they will be able to answer literal and inferential questions about the text with an accuracy rate of ninety percent or better. Their recollection of the text will include highlights, details, and an understanding of the author's purposes and subtle meanings.

Students who are reading below grade level fall into two categories: somewhat below and well below. Those who are reading somewhat below grade level will be able to decode grade-level text, but will experience some difficulty and will struggle with many words. They will have difficulty comprehending the text and will be able to answer fewer than seventy percent of the literal questions about a passage. They will answer far fewer inferential questions and will have difficulty recalling anything other than the most obvious elements of the text.

A small group of students can be characterized as reading well below grade level. They will have difficulty decoding many of the words in the text, their comprehension will be minimal, and they will be able to answer only a small percentage of literal questions about what they have read. They will recall little of the text, and as a result, will not understand critical elements like the role of characters or the plot.

Overview for Experienced Teachers

Intervention strategies can be implemented through individual, small-group, or whole-class instruction using *Open Court Reading* and its components. If a student is having reading difficulties and you have a hunch about what the problem might be, choose two or three assessments that are most appropriate for the time of year and the problem you suspect. Administer the assessments, score them according to the guidelines, and compare your hunch to the results. You can confirm your observation by administering a second assessment in the same or a related area. Here are some scenarios that will help you understand this procedure.

Scenario 1: Johnny is in fourth grade and is slipping further and further behind his peers in grasping the basics of reading. His failure to read is affecting his attitude toward school and his behavior in class. In this situation, you can be relatively confident that Johnny is having difficulty with all aspects of reading, from decoding through comprehension. Because he may be intimidated by any kind of assessment in which he is likely to fail, start with the Oral Word Reading assessment for the beginning of the year. Instead of having him read the words, however, ask him to scan the words to see if there are any he knows. He will probably be able to recognize a few of the words, so you will have an opportunity to take notes about the spelling patterns he recognizes, such as regular consonants, regular short and long vowels, and the like. This introductory assessment will build Johnny's confidence and help you understand his decoding strengths. Over the next few days, continue with other assessments, but you should do most of the reading and let Johnny answer orally. The results of the assessments will serve as a good point at which to start an intervention, which in Johnny's case will probably be small-group instruction to complement the whole-class instruction he is receiving already. For example, you may find it useful to spend fifteen minutes or so with Johnny's group previewing a lesson in *Open Court Reading* using the "Preview and Prepare" text. In addition, you may choose to administer the relevant skills assessments to this small group and interact with them about the information they used to choose their answers. The most important consideration with Johnny and students with similar characteristics is to minimize opportunities for failure and frustration while gradually increasing the level of challenge.

Scenario 2: Maria, a fifth grader whose first language is Spanish, seems to do as well as her peers when she reads orally. However, her achievement test scores from the previous year put her in the lower quartile of the class, and she gets only one or two questions correct in the *Open Court Reading Unit Assessment* or *Program Assessment* that deal with silent reading comprehension. Perhaps the best way to gain an understanding of Maria's problem is to choose a Silent Reading Comprehension assessment appropriate for the time of year and have her read the selection out loud. She should then choose an answer orally and explain the part of the selection that helped her answer the question. This process will confirm your estimation of her oral fluency in English and give you an idea of her ability to build understanding from text. If she struggles with the questions, then a good intervention strategy is to supplement the regular *Open Court Reading* instruction with individual or small-group instruction in which she reads orally and the two of you together, or with the assistance of Maria's peers, develop strategies for answering questions. You should also refer to the *English-Language Development Guide* and focus on activities that will enhance Maria's ability to internalize the meaning of the text that she is reading.

Scenario 3: Steve is a sixth grader who shows little interest in reading school assignments. He occasionally reads comic books or the sports page, but he struggles with grade-appropriate books. He will sometimes succeed with hi-lo books if they match his interests. The place to begin with Steve is to administer the beginning of the year Oral Fluency Assessment. The assessment will likely show that Steve is having a problem decoding and recognizing familiar words, so his reading rate will be slow, he will struggle over many words, and he will be able to derive only surface meaning from text. The best intervention for Steve is to review basic phonics skills in an age-appropriate way, teach him how to use structural analysis to understand longer words, and engage in "reading with" strategies. "Reading with" means that you or another capable reader would spend time reading orally with Steve. Both you and Steve should begin together. Then, as his confidence builds, he can try the text alone. If he stumbles over a word or two, then you can begin reading with him again. This strategy is most successful when Steve has an opportunity to choose books that match his interests and he is not made to feel that he is less capable than the other students in the class. In addition to this intervention, you should consider using either *Reteach* or the *Intervention Guide* along with the *Intervention Blackline Masters Book,* both of which will recommend activities you can use with Steve alone or in a small group of students with similar characteristics.

Diagnosing Students in Grades Four Through Six

Begin with the Oral Fluency Assessment for the beginning of the year. If students are clearly having reading difficulties, this relatively easy passage may be within their instructional level. If it is the beginning of the year, you may choose to drop down a grade level and administer the Oral Fluency Assessment of your choice from the previous grade. You may extend the Oral Fluency Assessment by asking questions about the passage that will give you insight into the student's comprehension of what was read.

Follow the Oral Fluency Assessment with a Vocabulary assessment and Silent Reading Comprehension assessment. You may either have the student attempt these assessments independently while working silently, or have the student complete the assessments orally with you available to provide any assistance that is necessary. The oral administration will give you a chance to observe the student's reading behaviors.

Applying the Results of Diagnostic Assessment

The results of the diagnostic assessments should help you determine the reading problem and identify areas of strength. As stated earlier, the most likely problems involve:

- Decoding or fluency
- Oral or silent reading comprehension
- Vocabulary development

It would be wonderful if every teacher had the time to work one-on-one with every student who is having reading difficulties, but this expectation is unrealistic. How, then, can a typical teacher use the results of a diagnosis to undertake appropriate remedial strategies?

The first step is to spend at least 15 minutes during Workshop with a small group of students who are having similar reading problems. One possibility is to "borrow" time during the period when students are expected to read on their own; for example, during a period of sustained silent reading.

Next, review the Teacher's Edition of **Open Court Reading** for strategies that will help resolve the problem you identified through the diagnosis. For example, consider a student in fourth grade who can decode well but still has comprehension difficulties. It would be relatively simple and extremely helpful to review the section of the teacher's guide entitled "Discussing the Selection" with this student and two or three peers with a similar problem. This section presents a series of questions relating to a reading selection in the **Open Court Reading** series. You can have the students read the selection orally with your support and then respond to the questions orally. Based on their responses, you can ask them to describe the strategy they used to answer the question, or you can suggest a more efficient strategy.

The various components of **Open Court Reading** will also provide you with support to help you capitalize on students' strengths and bolster their weaknesses. Some considerations to keep in mind when using these components are:

- For students who are having difficulty reading English because it is not their first language, turn to the **English-Language Development Guide.** This guide can be used to provide extra help with the vocabulary and sentence structure found in each **Open Court Reading** selection.

- For students who are reading more or less on level but are having difficulty with a specific skill or group of related skills, it makes the most sense to use the **Reteach** component. This resource offers additional practice in the skills that are featured in each **Open Court Reading Comprehension and Language Art Skills** lesson. It will also be helpful to group students who are having similar difficulties for instruction in these skills through brief, targeted lessons. For example, a small group might be developed to work on drawing conclusions. Once this instruction has been completed, the group should be disbanded to avoid the problem of ability grouping or tracking.

Skill grouping serves a clear instructional purpose, and students should become accustomed to moving in and out of small groups, depending on their learning needs at a given time.

- When students are clearly struggling and are falling further and further behind the rest of the class, the *Intervention Guide* and the *Intervention Blackline Masters Book* are the best resources to use. These materials give you an opportunity to preteach important skills to individuals or small groups of students before you undertake the whole-class instruction provided in *Open Court Reading*. Such preteaching increases the likelihood that struggling students will be able to master essential skills and catch up with the rest of the class.

The approaches described above are both efficient and effective, and they can be implemented without difficulty. They involve a reasonable use of your time and the students', require only the resources that are available to you, and allow you to focus on the reading behaviors in which students need additional instruction and practice.

Using the Assessments with New Students

The majority of students begin and end the school year in the same class. However, some students may move into the classroom during the school year. In some instances, this number may be relatively large. In order to use *Open Court Reading* most successfully with these students, it is important to know what their reading capabilities are. The assessments in this guide are ideally suited for this purpose, as well as for spot checking existing students on Oral Word Reading, Listening Comprehension, etc.

I. **If You Have Current Student Records:** Begin by evaluating the information that is available on the new student. If you have notes from the previous teacher, grades, achievement tests, test scores, or other sources of information, you should be able to estimate the student's reading ability with some confidence. From the available information you should determine whether the student is above average, average, below average in the same grade, or below average in a lower grade. When current student records are available, follow these steps:

    A. For students who are in **fourth, fifth, or sixth grade and are reading at an average or above-average level,** the purpose of the assessment is to confirm your estimated reading ability based on available information. Choose a Silent Reading Comprehension assessment. Follow the directions for administering and scoring the reading assessment.

        1. If the student's performance on the assessment is equal to or higher than your estimate, then undertake the same instructional practices you would with other students of the same ability level. You might also consider using activities from the *Challenge* component or providing this student with additional independent reading activities.

2. If the student's performance on the assessment is below your estimate, administer another Silent Reading Comprehension assessment. If the student's performance on the second assessment improves meaningfully, then tentatively assume the student is reading about the same as the other students in the class. If the student's performance is again less than you thought, follow the suggestions made in the previous section of this guide: **Diagnosing Students in Grades Four Through Six.** These suggestions will help you pinpoint the source of the student's reading difficulty.

B. For students who are in **fourth, fifth, or sixth grade and are reading below average,** the purpose of the assessment is to determine whether the student is reading well enough to benefit from the typical instructional practices you are following for students of comparable ability. Choose the Oral Fluency Assessment corresponding to the time of year the student entered the classroom (beginning, middle, or end). Follow the directions for administering and scoring the reading assessment.

1. If the student's performance on the assessment is equal to or higher than your estimate, then undertake the same instructional practices you would with other students of the same ability level. You may want to pay careful attention to this student's performance on the *Unit Assessment* and *Program Assessment* to make sure the student doesn't begin to slip behind the class as the level of reading challenge is increased.

2. If the student's performance on the assessment is below your estimate, follow the suggestions made in the previous section of this guide: **Diagnosing Students in Grades Four Through Six.** These suggestions will help you pinpoint the source of the student's reading difficulty. You may also want to use *Reteach* or *Intervention Guide* components with the students.

II. **If You Do Not Have Current Student Records:** The process of estimating a student's reading ability without prior information involves at least one extra step, but otherwise is similar to the procedures described above.

A. For students who are in **fourth, fifth, or sixth grade,** begin by administering the Oral Word Reading assessment corresponding to the time of year the student entered the classroom (beginning, middle, or end).

1. If the student struggles with this assessment, follow up with the appropriate Vocabulary assessment, but have the student complete it orally while you listen. Depending on his or her performance, you may either undertake the same instructional practices you would with other students of the same ability level or refer to the suggestions made in the previous section of this guide: **Diagnosing Students in Grades Four Through Six.** You may want to use *Reteach* or *Intervention Guide* components with these students.

2. If the student does well on these assessments, then follow up with one more assessment of your choosing. Based on the student's performance on this assessment, you should undertake the same instructional practices you would with other students of the same ability level, including the use of the ***Challenge*** component.

Oral Word Reading Introduction
Oral Fluency Introduction
Student Record
Assessment Summary

Oral Word Reading Introduction

The Oral Word Reading assessment is a simple and effective screening tool. By having students read relatively common words, you can gain an understanding of their ability to apply phonetic principles or to read sight words that are not readily decoded. This type of assessment is particularly useful with young students or older students who are reading well below grade level.

The words used in the Oral Word Reading assessments are drawn from the 1000 most common words found in text that students are likely to read. In addition to frequency, words were chosen because they are phonetically regular (*bed*), are phonetically irregular but common (*the*), or contain elements that can assist in the diagnosis of a reading problem (reading the word *down* as *do win*). Words have been placed in grades, and levels within grades, based on their phonetic patterns and overall frequency of use.

Each grade level's Oral Word Reading assessments can be found in the section of assessments for that particular grade level.

General Guidelines for Administration

The Oral Word Reading assessment has three levels, which correspond roughly to the beginning, middle, and end of the school year. Begin with the grade and level corresponding to the time of the school year the student enters the classroom. If you have a question about which assessment to use, choose the lower level rather than the higher level. If a student makes three or more errors in the first row of words, drop down to a lower level.

The Oral Word Reading assessment includes two pages for each assessment. The "Oral Word Reading: Student Prompt" page should be reproduced once and saved for use with multiple students. This page can be used often because students simply read the words from the page; they do not mark on it. The "Oral Word Reading: Student Record" page should be reproduced for each use. On this page, you will record the student's name, the date of the assessment, any errors the student made, and your observations during the assessment. A completed "Student Record" sample can be found on page 4.

Scoring and Interpreting the Oral Word Reading Assessment

The simplest way to score the Oral Word Reading assessment is to circle each word the student reads incorrectly, count the number of correct words, and then convert this score to a percentage. You can compare this percentage with the scores of other students on the same assessment or see how the percentage correct for the same student changes over time.

This simplified scoring can be greatly enhanced by recording the type of errors the student made and noting any behaviors that might indicate the student's reading difficulty. Shown below are some common errors and observations. This list is far from complete, but it will help you understand the importance of recording this additional information.

- Misreading regular vowels and consonants (reading *sat* as *sad* or *sit*, suggesting that the student needs instruction in decoding regular sounds)

- Mispronouncing an alternate consonant sound (pronouncing *his* as *hiss*, suggesting that the student needs instruction in alternate consonant sounds)

- Using phonetic principles to decode sight words (pronouncing *one* as *own*, suggesting that the student needs more direct instruction in sight words or the opportunity to read with a tutor who can point out these words in text)

- Depending on rudimentary syllabication rules to attack long or unfamiliar words (reading *something* as *so me thing*, suggesting that the student needs more supervised oral reading and familiarity with compound words)

- Mispronouncing diphthongs (reading *down* as *do win*, suggesting the student does not recall the correct pronunciation of the diphthong but is able to substitute high-frequency, regular words for the target word)

- Hesitating before each word but reading most of them correctly (suggesting the student has good reading skills but lacks confidence and probably will not read connected text fluently)

- Self-correcting often, even with fully decodable words (suggesting the student has not yet mastered decoding or recognizing sight words and will probably feel frustrated when reading silently)

- Reading confidently with a high error rate by substituting similar words (reading *more* as *move* or *were* as *wear*, suggesting that the student has reasonable decoding skills, is familiar with high-frequency words, and has a well-developed vocabulary, but is impulsive and could benefit from oral reading with instructional support)

As these examples show, the interpretation of the Oral Word Reading assessment is a straightforward undertaking. As a rule, the simplest interpretations, leading to practical interventions, are appropriate. Feel free to use your expertise and experience to administer the assessment and interpret the results in a way that is most consistent with your use of *Open Court Reading,* the needs of your students, and your available resources.

Sample
Oral Word Reading: Student Record
Fourth Grade (Beginning of year)

Name __Bart Gianni__   Date __10/4__

which	to	very	*fast* ~~first~~	way
after	*come* ~~came~~	right	*who* ~~how~~	life
care	everyone	sound	within	*looked* ~~looking~~
given	*older* ~~order~~	high	animal	understand

Directions

Duplicate page 19 and give it to the student. Duplicate this page and use it as a Student Record for scoring and noting your observations.

Say: Here are some words I would like you to read for me. Read each row of words. If you are not sure how to read a word, take your best guess. You may begin now.

As the student reads, circle each word the student reads wrong. If possible, note the type of error, for example, reading *made* as *mad*. Also, observe the student as she or he reads and record any relevant observations in the space below.

Fourth Grade (Beginning of year)

20 Words   **Number Correct** __15__   **Percent Correct** __75__

(Multiply the number of correct words by 5 to find the percent correct.)

Observations

__Bart seemed to read impulsively rather than looking at the words carefully. I'm going to test__

__him again in a few weeks and try to get him to take his time.__

Diagnostic Assessment

Oral Fluency Introduction

The Oral Fluency Assessment is one of the teacher's most powerful means for evaluating students' ability to read. It is simple to administer and score, yet provides extraordinarily useful quantitative and qualitative data.

The readability of the stories is at the low end of a given grade. The words in the stories are of sufficient variety to allow a teacher to analyze the decoding and vocabulary abilities of a student and draw inferences about the student's ability to derive meaning from the text.

General Guidelines for Administration

The Oral Fluency Assessment has three levels, corresponding roughly to the beginning, middle, and end of the school year. If you have a question about which assessment to use, choose the lower level rather than the higher level. If a student misreads at least half of the words in the first few sentences of the assessment, drop down one grade lower than a student's current grade placement.

The Oral Fluency Assessment includes two pages for each assessment. The "Oral Fluency Assessment: Student Prompt" page should be reproduced once and saved for use with multiple students. This page can be used often because students simply read the words from the page; they do not mark on it. The "Oral Fluency Assessment: Student Record" page should be reproduced for each use. On this page, you will record the student's name, the date of the assessment, and the results of the assessment. A completed "Student Record" sample can be found on page 8.

Administering, Scoring, and Interpreting the Oral Fluency Assessment

Duplicate the "Student Record" and fill in the name and date information. Give the "Student Prompt" to the student with the following directions:

Say: Here is a story I would like you to read out loud for me. I am going to listen to you read and take some notes. The notes I take will help me learn how well you can read. You will not be graded for this, so you should not feel nervous. Read the story carefully and do your best. Take a few minutes now to look over the story, and then I will tell you when to begin.

Allow time for the student to preview the story. Be sure you have a pen or pencil, the "Student Record," a stopwatch or other timer, and any other materials you may need.

Say: Are you ready? (Check to be sure the student is ready.) You may begin now.

Start the timer or watch as the student begins to read. You may pronounce any proper nouns with which the student is unfamiliar. Do not count these words as errors.

Note: If the student becomes frustrated or makes several consecutive errors, stop the assessment.

At the end of one minute, draw a box around the last word the student reads. If the student is reading with acceptable fluency and you have time available, allow the student to finish the text. As the student reads, draw a line through each word that is misread. If possible, note each type of error the student makes.

These guidelines will help you score the student's performance accurately:

- Self-correcting should not be counted as an error.
- Repeating the same mistake should be counted as only one error.
- Hesitating for more than five seconds (teacher should then provide the word) should count as an error.
- Become familiar with the evaluating codes before administering the Oral Fluency Assessment.
- Draw a line through any word that is misread. Count this as an error. If possible, note the type of error (misreading "short a" as "short e," reading "get" as "jet," and so on).
- Draw a box around the last word the student reads in one minute.
- Circle words the student omits or refuses to read and count them as errors, even if you prompt the student.
- Indicate extra words that have been inserted with a caret. If possible, write the inserted word. Count insertions as errors.
- Draw an arrow between words that have been reversed. Count these as one error.
- Put two check marks above a word the student repeats. Do not count this as an error.

To find the student's accuracy rate:

Count the total number of words read in one minute. The numbers beside the passage in the Teacher's Annotated Edition will make this an easier task. Subtract the number of errors from the total number of words read, and use that figure to find the number of correct words read per minute. Then, divide the correct words per minute by the total number of words to get the correct rate. Record these numbers on the Reading Rate and Accuracy chart.

- Record the student's scores on the Oral Fluency Scores chart, found in the Unit Assessments, and the Student Record. The Student Record and the Oral Fluency Scores can be kept in the student's Cumulative Folder.
- Complete the Reading Fluency scale at the bottom of the page. These qualitative measures indicate your subjective judgment of how the student compares with other students in the same grade.

To interpret the Oral Fluency Assessments:

First, compare the student's number of correct words per minute with the following chart. This will give you an idea of how the student compares with other students in the same grade at the same time of year. The data in the chart represents the approximate fluency rate a student should attain periodically in grade 2–6. The two rows of numbers represent the 50th and the 75th percentiles.

	Unit 1	Unit 2	Unit 3	Unit 4	Unit 5	Unit 6	
Grade 2	82	90	98	106	115	124	75th percentile
	53	61	70	78	86	94	50th percentile
Grade 3	107	112	118	123	133	142	75th percentile
	79	84	88	93	104	114	50th percentile
Grade 4	125	128	130	133	138	143	75th percentile
	99	103	108	112	115	118	50th percentile
Grade 5	126	132	137	143	147	151	75th percentile
	105	109	114	118	123	128	50th percentile
Grade 6	145	150	155	160	165	170	75th percentile
	125	132	138	145	148	150	50th percentile

Source Adapted from "Curriculum-Based Oral Reading Fluency Norms for Students Grades 2 through 5" (1992) by Jan E. Hasbrouck and Gerald Tindal. *Teaching Exceptional Children*, Vol. 24 (Spring).

Then, examine the student's accuracy percentage. Reading accuracy should remain constant or gradually increase within a grade and between grades, until it stabilizes at 90 percent or higher. You may find it helpful to compare the student's accuracy percentage after each administration to ensure that it is remaining constant or increasing.

Next, examine the types of errors the student is making, and consider how they represent the underlying reading behaviors. Here are some examples:

- Inserting extra words suggests that the student understands what is read, is constructing meaning, but is reading somewhat impulsively.

- A student who refuses to attempt a word is probably uncertain of his or her abilities and is unwilling to take risks.

- Misreading regular letter sounds implies that the student has not yet mastered the conventions of the sound-symbol relationship. This is in contrast with the student who misreads complex letter sounds (alternate sounds, blends, diphthongs, digraphs) but has little difficulty with regular letter sounds.

Finally, consider the error pattern. If errors are scattered randomly throughout the passage, then the error types represent skills the student has not yet developed. If errors increase in frequency from beginning to end, then fatigue or inattention are involved.

As a follow-up to the Oral Fluency Assessment, ask the student questions about the passage. The questions should focus on skills such as main idea, characters, setting, details, inferences, summaries, and conclusions.

Sample
Oral Fluency Assessment: Student Record
Fifth Grade (Beginning of year)

Name **Layla Miller**   Date **10/27**

Building a Country

self-correct
cooperation

One of the best examples of ~~cooperation~~ in history is the United States. The   1–14
United States was born more than two hundred years ago. It happened because   15–27
people were willing to cooperate. It ~~survives~~ today for the same reason.   28–39

Long ago, America was controlled by European countries. One of these   40–50
~~countries~~ was England. The people in America decided to band together and   51–62
form a new country that was independent. The people living in America   63–74
inserted
had come from many different ^ places and had different interests. Even so, **kinds of**   75–86
they joined forces and ~~fought~~ a war for independence from England. They   87–98
won the war, but now they faced an even greater task—building a new country.   99–113

After the war, the people formed a new ~~government~~ that ~~depended~~ on **officers**   114–125
cooperation. People in each state would vote for ~~officials~~ such as a president,   126–138
a governor, and senators. Whoever got the most votes would win the election.   139–151
The people who voted had to cooperate and support the officials who were   152–164
elected. This kind of cooperation was ~~unusual~~ at that time, but it worked. **usual**   165–177

The biggest ~~challenge~~ to the United States came during the Civil War.   178–189
The states in the South wanted to leave the United States. The states in   190–203
the North didn't want this. They fought a war that the North won. After   204–217
inserted
the war, the people once more cooperated, and the country was united ^ **States**   218–229
again. Since that time, people have had different ~~opinions.~~ They still   230–240
cooperate with one another, ~~however,~~ and today America is a wonderful   241–251
| place | to live.   **whoever**   252–254

EVALUATING CODES
FOR ORAL FLUENCY

sky   (/) words read incorrectly

blue
^   sky   (^) inserted word
          ( ]) after the last word

READING RATE AND ACCURACY

Total Words Read:	**254**
Number of Errors:	– **13**
Number of Correct Words Read Per Minute (WPM):	**241**
Accuracy Rate:	**95**

READING FLUENCY

	Low	Average	High
Decoding ability	○	●	○
Pace	○	●	○
Syntax	○	●	○
Self-correction	○	●	○
Intonation	○	●	○

Student Record and Assessment Summary

The "Student Record" form and the "Assessment Summary" form are used at each grade level with the diagnostic assessments. In order to draw conclusions from the assessments you administer, it will be helpful to summarize your data. The "Student Record" form on page 10 and the "Assessment Summary" form on page 11 will help you do this.

For each student and assessment, duplicate the "Student Record" form and fill in the form according to these guidelines:

- Fill in the student's name and the date of the assessment.
- Write the name of the assessment.
- Fill in the total number of items, the number correct, and the percentage correct.
- Record any student observations you made during the assessment, including student behavior and the results of the assessment.

Duplicate the "Assessment Summary" form for each student you assess. As you complete the assessments, fill in the form according to these guidelines:

- Fill in the student's name and grade.
- Write the name of the assessment, the date it was administered, and the percentage score the student earned. The chart on the inside back cover of this guide can be used to calculate percentage scores from number correct and the total number of items in an assessment.
- Write a brief summary of the results of the assessment and your observations, including intervention strategies you would like to implement with the student.

Keep the "Student Record" form, the "Assessment Summary" form, and completed assessments in the student's folder. If you conduct any additional assessments with the student, be sure to add them to the "Assessment Summary" form. Periodically throughout the school year, note any changes in the student's reading behaviors and describe the relative success of the interventions you implemented.

Student Record

Name _____ **Date** _____

Assessment _____

Total Number of Items _____ **Number Correct** _____ **Percentage Correct** _____

Observations:

_____

_____

_____

_____

_____

_____

_____

_____

_____

_____

_____

_____

_____

_____

_____

_____

_____

_____

_____

_____

_____

Diagnostic Assessment

Assessment Summary

Name _____ Date _____

Name of Assessment	Date	Percentage Score
_____	_____	_____
_____	_____	_____
_____	_____	_____
_____	_____	_____
_____	_____	_____
_____	_____	_____
_____	_____	_____

Summary and Observations

_____

_____

_____

_____

_____

_____

_____

_____

_____

_____

_____

_____

_____

Literacy Interview

Literacy Interview

A student's reading ability often is affected significantly by his or her literacy background. Unfortunately, this information is not readily available to most teachers. The interview form on pages 15–16 will help you gather this information, which you can then use to enhance your understanding of a student's reading abilities and weaknesses.

Duplicate the form each time you interview a student. Fill in the student's name and the date of the interview on the form. Then, ask the student the questions orally and record the student's responses in the spaces provided.

Before beginning, read the following text to the student. You may adapt the text to match the student's cognitive abilities.

Say: I'm going to ask you some questions about reading and books. This is not a test, and there are no right or wrong answers. I will write down your answers so I can remember them in the future. Your answers will help me decide what we can do to help you read better. Are you ready? Let's begin.

In addition to recording the student's responses, encourage the student to elaborate on any answers you think are especially meaningful. Record these extended responses, using the back of the form if necessary.

Because of the nature of this interview, there is no answer key. It is best to interpret the information from the interview in light of the student's reading behaviors.

Literacy Interview

Name _____ **Date**_____

1. What are some reasons that people read? _____
   _____
   _____

2. What are some books that you like to read? Can you remember their names?
   _____
   _____
   _____

3. Do you have favorite authors? Can you remember the names of authors who
   wrote your favorite books? _____
   _____

4. Do you own any books? How many do you have? _____
   _____

5. Are there books in your house? About how many books do you think there are?
   _____
   _____

6. Are there magazines and newspapers in your house? What are they about?
   _____
   _____

7. Do the people in your family read very often? _____
   _____

8. About how often do you read a book just for fun? Is it every day, once a week…?
   _____

9. Suppose you read a book and come upon a word you don't understand. What do
   you do? _____
   _____
   _____

10. Are there any books you like to read again and again? What are their names?

_____

_____

11. Do you like to talk about books with your friends? _____

(If Yes, follow with . . . What books do you talk about with your friends?)

_____

_____

12. Some people are good at sports, or singing, or other things. You know what makes these people good at what they do. What do you think makes a good reader? _____

_____

_____

13. Do you think you are a good reader? _____

Why do you think this? _____

_____

_____

14. How do you think most people learn to read? _____

_____

_____

15. Suppose you had a friend who didn't read very well. What could a teacher do to help your friend? _____

_____

_____

16. Think about your own reading. What could you do to be a better reader?

_____

_____

_____

Diagnostic Assessment

Oral Word Reading
Oral Fluency Assessment

Oral Word Reading

Specific instructions for administration are included with each Oral Word Reading assessment. Duplicate the "Student Record" page and give it to the student. Duplicate the scoring page for your use to record each student's scores and any observations.

For instructions on scoring and interpreting these assessments, see Oral Word Reading Introduction.

Oral Fluency Assessment

These directions will help you administer the Oral Fluency Assessments for fourth-grade students. Reproduce the "Student Prompt" page once and save it for use with multiple students. Reproduce the "Student Record" page for each student receiving the assessment. Fill in the name and date information. Give the "Student Prompt" to the student with the following directions:

Say: Here is a story I would like you to read out loud for me. I am going to listen to you read and take some notes. The notes I take will help me learn how well you can read. You will not be graded for this, so you should not feel nervous. Read the story carefully and do your best. Take a few minutes now to look over the story, and then I will tell you when to begin.

Allow time for the student to preview the story. Be sure you have a pen or pencil, the "Student Record," a stopwatch or other timer, and any other materials you may need.

Say: Are you ready? You may begin now.

Start the timer or watch as the student begins to read. You may pronounce any proper nouns with which the student is unfamiliar. Do not count these words as errors

As the student reads, draw a line through each word the student misreads. If possible, note each type of error the student makes by writing it on the "Student Record."

For specific instructions on scoring and interpreting these assessments, see Oral Fluency Introduction.

Oral Word Reading: Student Record
Fourth Grade (Beginning of year)

Name _____ Date _____

which	to	very	first	way
after	came	right	how	life
care	everyone	sound	within	looking
given	order	high	animal	understand

Directions

Duplicate page 20 and give it to the student. Duplicate this page and use it as a Student Record for scoring and noting your observations.

Say: Here are some words I would like you to read for me. Read each row of words. If you are not sure how to read a word, take your best guess. You may begin now.

As the student reads, circle each word the student reads wrong. If possible, note the type of error, for example, reading *made* as *mad*. Also, observe the student as she or he reads and record any relevant observations in the space below.

Fourth Grade (Beginning of year)

20 Words   **Number Correct** _____   **Percent Correct** _____

(Multiply the number of correct words by 5 to find the percent correct.)

Observations

_____

_____

_____

_____

_____

_____

Oral Word Reading: Student Prompt

which	to	very	first	way
after	came	right	how	life
care	everyone	sound	within	looking
given	order	high	animal	understand

   Diagnostic Assessment

Oral Word Reading: Student Record
Fourth Grade (Middle of year)

Name _____ Date _____

lived	known	today	almost	women
following	someone	using	finally	least
doing	instead	answer	ready	reason
carried	history	major	present	window

Directions

Duplicate page 22 and give it to the student. Duplicate this page and use it as a Student Record for scoring and noting your observations.

Say: Here are some words I would like you to read for me. Read each row of words. If you are not sure how to read a word, take your best guess. You may begin now.

As the student reads, circle each word the student reads wrong. If possible, note the type of error, for example, reading *made* as *mad*. Also, observe the student as she or he reads and record any relevant observations in the space below.

Fourth Grade (Middle of year)

20 Words   **Number Correct** _____   **Percent Correct** _____

(Multiply the number of correct words by 5 to find the percent correct.)

Observations

_____

_____

_____

_____

_____

Oral Word Reading: Student Prompt

lived	known	today	almost	women
following	someone	using	finally	least
doing	instead	answer	ready	reason
carried	history	major	present	window

    Diagnostic Assessment

Oral Word Reading: Student Record
Fourth Grade (End of year)

Name _____   Date _____

plant	outside	result	center	decided
field	question	hair	gone	hundred
start	force	else	beginning	national
suddenly	friend	president	natural	carefully

Directions

Duplicate page 24 and give it to the student. Duplicate this page and use it as a Student Record for scoring and noting your observations.

Say: Here are some words I would like you to read for me. Read each row of words. If you are not sure how to read a word, take your best guess. You may begin now.

As the student reads, circle each word the student reads wrong. If possible, note the type of error, for example, reading *made* as *mad*. Also, observe the student as she or he reads and record any relevant observations in the space below.

Fourth Grade (End of year)

20 Words   **Number Correct** _____   **Percent Correct** _____

(Multiply the number of correct words by 5 to find the percent correct.)

Observations

_____

_____

_____

_____

_____

_____

Oral Word Reading: Student Prompt

plant	outside	result	center	decided
field	question	hair	gone	hundred
start	force	else	beginning	national
suddenly	friend	president	natural	carefully

Diagnostic Assessment

Name _____ Date _____

Too Much for Shoes

Howard looked at all the shoes. They were all so expensive. He decided to save his money. He would buy shoes on sale later.

On the way home from the mall, he said to his mother, "Why are athletic shoes so expensive? Don't the people who make shoes know that kids don't have a lot of money?"

His mother thought for a minute before she answered. "You know," she said, "all athletic shoes aren't expensive. Only the ones that are very popular cost a lot of money. If you look around the store, you could probably find shoes that cost less."

"I know," replied Howard, "but those shoes aren't any good."

"I'm not so sure," said his mother. "Maybe that's what the people who make shoes want you to believe. That way, they can charge more for those shoes."

Howard thought for a minute. Then he said, "Mom, I never thought about that before. What kind of shoes do you run in? You are a good runner. Dad is a good runner, too. What kind of shoes does he wear? Do you buy the same kind of shoes that I do?"

"I'll tell you what," suggested Howard's mother, "let's turn around and go back to the mall. I'll show you the kind of shoes that I think are best for running. Then you can decide if that's the kind of shoes you want."

1–11
12–24
25–37
38–48
49–57
58–67
68–77
78–91
92–101
102–111
112–121
122–133
134–139
140–150
151–163
164–177
178–191
192–200
201–214
215–227
228–233

EVALUATING CODES FOR ORAL FLUENCY

sky   (/) words read incorrectly

blue
^   sky   (^) inserted word
              ( ]) after the last word

READING RATE AND ACCURACY

Total Words Read: _____

Number of Errors: − _____

Number of Correct Words
Read Per Minute (WPM):   _____

Accuracy Rate: _____

READING FLUENCY

	Low	Average	High
Decoding ability	◯	◯	◯
Pace	◯	◯	◯
Syntax	◯	◯	◯
Self-correction	◯	◯	◯
Intonation	◯	◯	◯

Too Much for Shoes

Howard looked at all the shoes. They were all so expensive. He decided to save his money. He would buy shoes on sale later.

On the way home from the mall, he said to his mother, "Why are athletic shoes so expensive? Don't the people who make shoes know that kids don't have a lot of money?"

His mother thought for a minute before she answered. "You know," she said, "all athletic shoes aren't expensive. Only the ones that are very popular cost a lot of money. If you look around the store, you could probably find shoes that cost less."

"I know," replied Howard, "but those shoes aren't any good."

"I'm not so sure," said his mother. "Maybe that's what the people who make shoes want you to believe. That way, they can charge more for those shoes."

Howard thought for a minute. Then he said, "Mom, I never thought about that before. What kind of shoes do you run in? You are a good runner. Dad is a good runner, too. What kind of shoes does he wear? Do you buy the same kind of shoes that I do?"

"I'll tell you what," suggested Howard's mother, "let's turn around and go back to the mall. I'll show you the kind of shoes that I think are best for running. Then you can decide if that's the kind of shoes you want."

Oral Fluency Assessment: Student Record
Fourth Grade (Middle of year)

Name _____ **Date** _____

Beating the Rain

The rain had been falling for days. The river was rising and
the Garcia family was beginning to be concerned about a flood.
They watched the news, but there was no weather warning.

Mr. and Mrs. Garcia discussed the storm with the children.
They decided to pack up as much as they could and go to Aunt
Maria's house for a while. She didn't live very far away.

Everyone was in the car and the bags were in the trunk. With
Mrs. Garcia at the wheel, they pulled out of the garage into the
storm. She drove cautiously, avoiding the sections of the road
where the water might be too deep. As the car turned the corner,
everyone glanced back at the house. They didn't know if it would
be there when they returned.

When they came to the bridge over the river, Mrs. Garcia stopped
the car because the water was actually up to the bridge. Mr. Garcia
got out and trudged across the bridge ahead of the car. He wanted
to make sure there were no sections of the bridge that were too deep.
When he got back in the car, the children all cheered for Mr. Garcia.

At last, they reached the other side and high ground. They were
going to be all right. In just fifteen minutes they would arrive at Aunt
Maria's house where it was warm, dry, and safe.

1–12
13–23
24–33
34–43
44–57
58–68
69–81
82–94
95–104
105–117
118–129
130–134
135–146
147–159
160–172
173–186
187–200
201–212
213–226
227–235

EVALUATING CODES FOR ORAL FLUENCY

sky   (/) words read incorrectly

blue
^   sky   (^) inserted word
              ( ]) after the last word

READING RATE AND ACCURACY

Total Words Read: _____

Number of Errors: − _____

Number of Correct Words
Read Per Minute (WPM):   _____

Accuracy Rate: _____

READING FLUENCY

	Low	Average	High
Decoding ability	○	○	○
Pace	○	○	○
Syntax	○	○	○
Self-correction	○	○	○
Intonation	○	○	○

Beating the Rain

The rain had been falling for days. The river was rising and the Garcia family was beginning to be concerned about a flood. They watched the news, but there was no weather warning.

Mr. and Mrs. Garcia discussed the storm with the children. They decided to pack up as much as they could and go to Aunt Maria's house for a while. She didn't live very far away.

Everyone was in the car and the bags were in the trunk. With Mrs. Garcia at the wheel, they pulled out of the garage into the storm. She drove cautiously, avoiding the sections of the road where the water might be too deep. As the car turned the corner, everyone glanced back at the house. They didn't know if it would be there when they returned.

When they came to the bridge over the river, Mrs. Garcia stopped the car because the water was actually up to the bridge. Mr. Garcia got out and trudged across the bridge ahead of the car. He wanted to make sure there were no sections of the bridge that were too deep. When he got back in the car, the children all cheered for Mr. Garcia.

At last, they reached the other side and high ground. They were going to be all right. In just fifteen minutes they would arrive at Aunt Maria's house where it was warm, dry, and safe.

Oral Fluency Assessment: Student Record
Fourth Grade (End of year)

Name _____ **Date** _____

The Old Days

The phone rang and Karen picked it up. It was her grandmother
who called to say hello and see how Karen was doing. Karen spoke
with her grandmother for a few minutes and then hung up the phone.

A few minutes later, Karen asked her mother, "Mom, when you
were my age, did you talk to your grandmother every week? I think it
is wonderful that Grandma and I talk so often."

Mrs. Allen stopped what she was doing and answered, "Karen, when
I was your age, we didn't even have a telephone. My mother and father
didn't think we needed one. It's funny, but I think they were right. If
there was an emergency, we could go next door to the Nelsons. But
other than that, we really didn't need a telephone."

Karen looked at her mother for a minute and then asked, "How did
you talk to your friends? How did you talk to your grandmother? And
how did you order things? How did you get pizza?"

"Let's see," answered Mrs. Allen, "I talked to my friends at school, and
that was enough. Gran, that's what I called my grandmother, lived
around the corner. We just walked over to her house. And as for ordering
things, there was nothing to order. If you wanted pizza, you walked to
Tony's Restaurant. He made the best pizza in town."

"Mom," said Karen, "I can't wait to go to school tomorrow. When I tell
everyone how you lived without a telephone, no one will believe me."

1–12
13–25
26–38
39–49
50–63
64–72
73–83
84–97
98–111
112–124
125–133
134–146
147–159
160–169
170–182
183–193
194–207
208–220
221–229
230–243
244–255

EVALUATING CODES FOR ORAL FLUENCY

sky   (/) words read incorrectly

blue

^   sky   (^) inserted word

            ( ]) after the last word

READING RATE AND ACCURACY

Total Words Read: _____

Number of Errors: − _____

Number of Correct Words
Read Per Minute (WPM): _____

Accuracy Rate: _____

READING FLUENCY

	Low	Average	High
Decoding ability	○	○	○
Pace	○	○	○
Syntax	○	○	○
Self-correction	○	○	○
Intonation	○	○	○

The Old Days

The phone rang and Karen picked it up. It was her grandmother who called to say hello and see how Karen was doing. Karen spoke with her grandmother for a few minutes and then hung up the phone.

A few minutes later, Karen asked her mother, "Mom, when you were my age, did you talk to your grandmother every week? I think it is wonderful that Grandma and I talk so often."

Mrs. Allen stopped what she was doing and answered, "Karen, when I was your age, we didn't even have a telephone. My mother and father didn't think we needed one. It's funny, but I think they were right. If there was an emergency, we could go next door to the Nelsons. But other than that, we really didn't need a telephone."

Karen looked at her mother for a minute and then asked, "How did you talk to your friends? How did you talk to your grandmother? And how did you order things? How did you get pizza?"

"Let's see," answered Mrs. Allen, "I talked to my friends at school, and that was enough. Gran, that's what I called my grandmother, lived around the corner. We just walked over to her house. And as for ordering things, there was nothing to order. If you wanted pizza, you walked to Tony's Restaurant. He made the best pizza in town."

"Mom," said Karen, "I can't wait to go to school tomorrow. When I tell everyone how you lived without a telephone, no one will believe me."

Spelling

Spelling

The assessments in this section are intended to be completed by a student working independently. The pages for these assessments should be duplicated and distributed to the student. You may find it helpful to read the directions for these assessments out loud before they are administered to ensure that the student understands what to do.

Duplicate the "Student Record" form on page 10 and complete the record for each assessment. You can calculate the percentage correct by hand or look it up in the percentage chart on the inside back cover of this guide. The "Student Record" has space for you to record the observations you make while the student is completing the assessment. Note things such as the speed with which the student works, signs of frustration, attempts at self-correction, and other relevant behaviors.

If some students are having difficulty reading, you may choose to administer the assessments orally. One possibility is to read the assessment to the student and have the student fill in the correct answer. Another possibility is to read the assessment with the student. Allow the student to begin reading, and when the student encounters difficulty, read along with the student until he or she begins reading fluently again.

You may enhance either method of assessment—student reading silently or with your assistance—by asking the student questions like "How do you know that?" or "What makes you sure this answer is right?" The student's answers to these follow-up questions can give you further insight into his or her understanding of the task and his or her ability to read with understanding.

The following chart provides an assessment guideline for each of the fourth-grade Spelling assessments.

Assessment	Estimated Percentiles		
	0–49	50–79	80+
Spelling the /er/ Sound (p. 33)	0–5	6–8	9–10
Short Vowels (p. 35)	0–5	6–8	9–10
Regular and Irregular Plurals (p. 37)	0–5	6–8	9–10
Final -le, -el, -al, -il, or -ol (p. 39)	0–5	6–8	9–10
Long-Vowel Spelling Patterns (p. 41)	0–5	6–8	9–10
Frequently Misspelled Words (p. 43)	0–5	6–8	9–10

Spelling the /er/ Sound

**Read each sentence. Fill in the circle beside the word
that is spelled correctly and fits best in the blank.**

1. Our vacation turned into an _____ .
   ○ adventure   ○ adventere   ○ adventore

2. Jennie's _____ test score is improving.
   ○ avurage   ○ avarage   ○ average

3. Without his glasses, Ben's vision is _____ .
   ○ blurry   ○ blerry   ○ blorry

4. The _____ will come to town next month.
   ○ circus   ○ curcus   ○ cercus

5. George _____ the soup after adding pepper.
   ○ sterred   ○ sturred   ○ stirred

6. This book was written by my favorite _____ .
   ○ auther   ○ author   ○ authur

7. Put the _____ dishes in the sink.
   ○ derty   ○ durty   ○ dirty

8. Are you _____ this is the right street?
   ○ curtain   ○ cirtain   ○ certain

9. Mrs. Cox is a _____ teacher.
   ○ popular   ○ populer   ○ populur

10. The river makes a big _____ through our town.
    ○ cerve   ○ curve   ○ cirve

Spelling the /er/ Sound

**Read each sentence. Fill in the circle beside the word
that is spelled correctly and fits best in the blank.**

1. Our vacation turned into an _____ .
   - ● adventure
   - ○ adventere
   - ○ adventore

2. Jennie's _____ test score is improving.
   - ○ avurage
   - ○ avarage
   - ● average

3. Without his glasses, Ben's vision is _____ .
   - ● blurry
   - ○ blerry
   - ○ blorry

4. The _____ will come to town next month.
   - ● circus
   - ○ curcus
   - ○ cercus

5. George _____ the soup after adding pepper.
   - ○ sterred
   - ○ sturred
   - ● stirred

6. This book was written by my favorite _____ .
   - ○ auther
   - ● author
   - ○ authur

7. Put the _____ dishes in the sink.
   - ○ derty
   - ○ durty
   - ● dirty

8. Are you _____ this is the right street?
   - ○ curtain
   - ○ cirtain
   - ● certain

9. Mrs. Cox is a _____ teacher.
   - ● popular
   - ○ populer
   - ○ populur

10. The river makes a big _____ through our town.
   - ○ cerve
   - ● curve
   - ○ cirve

Diagnostic Assessment

Name _____   Date _____

Short Vowels

**Read each word. Fill in the circle under the word
that has only short-vowel sounds.**

1. neither   afraid   except
   ○   ○   ○

2. subject   playing   before
   ○   ○   ○

3. ocean   beside   finish
   ○   ○   ○

4. crying   hundred   sometimes
   ○   ○   ○

5. follow   basket   remember
   ○   ○   ○

6. telephone   dream   added
   ○   ○   ○

7. within   myself   meeting
   ○   ○   ○

8. paper   extra   higher
   ○   ○   ○

9. object   surprise   tonight
   ○   ○   ○

10. seaside   cupcake   pocket
    ○   ○   ○

Short Vowels

Read each word. Fill in the circle under the word that has only short-vowel sounds.

1. neither   afraid   except
   ○   ○   ●

2. subject   playing   before
   ●   ○   ○

3. ocean   beside   finish
   ○   ○   ●

4. crying   hundred   sometimes
   ○   ●   ○

5. follow   basket   remember
   ○   ●   ○

6. telephone   dream   added
   ○   ○   ●

7. within   myself   meeting
   ●   ○   ○

8. paper   extra   higher
   ○   ●   ○

9. object   surprise   tonight
   ●   ○   ○

10. seaside   cupcake   pocket
    ○   ○   ●

Diagnostic Assessment

Regular and Irregular Plurals

Read each sentence. Fill in the circle next to the correctly spelled plural word that fits best in each blank.

1. Both _____ were packed with people.
   ○ beach   ○ beaches   ○ beachs

2. There are four _____ in one gallon.
   ○ quartes   ○ quarties   ○ quarts

3. This week, Jerome will go to three _____.
   ○ partys   ○ partyes   ○ parties

4. Three of the _____ are still in the barn.
   ○ ponies   ○ ponys   ○ poneys

5. In autumn, the _____ of many kinds of trees change color.
   ○ leaves   ○ leafs   ○ leafes

6. The cows at the dairy farm had a total of six _____ this year.
   ○ calfes   ○ calfe   ○ calves

7. How many _____ will be going to the dance?
   ○ mans   ○ men   ○ mens

8. Sixteen _____ flew over the house.
   ○ geese   ○ gooses   ○ goosies

9. Three _____ were performed during the concert.
   ○ solo   ○ soloes   ○ solos

10. Paul caught four _____ on Saturday and released all of them.
    ○ fish   ○ fishees   ○ fishs

Diagnostic Assessment   **37**

Regular and Irregular Plurals

Read each sentence. Fill in the circle next to the correctly spelled plural word that fits best in each blank.

1. Both _____ were packed with people.
   - ○ beach
   - ● beaches
   - ○ beachs

2. There are four _____ in one gallon.
   - ○ quartes
   - ○ quarties
   - ● quarts

3. This week, Jerome will go to three _____.
   - ○ partys
   - ○ partyes
   - ● parties

4. Three of the _____ are still in the barn.
   - ● ponies
   - ○ ponys
   - ○ poneys

5. In autumn, the _____ of many kinds of trees change color.
   - ● leaves
   - ○ leafs
   - ○ leafes

6. The cows at the dairy farm had a total of six _____ this year.
   - ○ calfes
   - ○ calfe
   - ● calves

7. How many _____ will be going to the dance?
   - ○ mans
   - ● men
   - ○ mens

8. Sixteen _____ flew over the house.
   - ● geese
   - ○ gooses
   - ○ goosies

9. Three _____ were performed during the concert.
   - ○ solo
   - ○ soloes
   - ● solos

10. Paul caught four _____ on Saturday and released all of them.
    - ● fish
    - ○ fishees
    - ○ fishs

Final *-le, -el, -al, -il,* or *-ol*

Read each sentence. Fill in the circle next to the word that correctly completes that sentence.

1. The family stayed at a nice _____ .
   - ○ hotl
   - ○ hotel
   - ○ hotle

2. My _____ needs to be sharpened.
   - ○ pencil
   - ○ pencel
   - ○ pencle

3. This is a good _____ of how to solve the problem.
   - ○ exampel
   - ○ exampil
   - ○ example

4. Make sure that board is _____ .
   - ○ level
   - ○ levle
   - ○ levil

5. What was the _____ bill?
   - ○ totol
   - ○ total
   - ○ totel

6. How many _____ are going to the picnic?
   - ○ people
   - ○ peopel
   - ○ peopll

7. The _____ goes under the river.
   - ○ tunnil
   - ○ tunnle
   - ○ tunnel

8. We will take a tour of the _____ building.
   - ○ Capitol
   - ○ Capitel
   - ○ Capitul

9. This is the _____ way to fix that tire.
   - ○ simpil
   - ○ simpel
   - ○ simple

10. My mother works at the _____ .
    - ○ hospitol
    - ○ hospital
    - ○ hospitle

Final -*le*, -*el*, -*al*, -*il*, or -*ol*

Read each sentence. Fill in the circle next to the word that correctly completes that sentence.

1. The family stayed at a nice _____ .
   - ○ hotl
   - ● hotel
   - ○ hotle

2. My _____ needs to be sharpened.
   - ● pencil
   - ○ pencel
   - ○ pencle

3. This is a good _____ of how to solve the problem.
   - ○ exampel
   - ○ exampil
   - ● example

4. Make sure that board is _____ .
   - ● level
   - ○ levle
   - ○ levil

5. What was the _____ bill?
   - ○ totol
   - ● total
   - ○ totel

6. How many _____ are going to the picnic?
   - ● people
   - ○ peopel
   - ○ peopll

7. The _____ goes under the river.
   - ○ tunnil
   - ○ tunnle
   - ● tunnel

8. We will take a tour of the _____ building.
   - ● Capitol
   - ○ Capitel
   - ○ Capitul

9. This is the _____ way to fix that tire.
   - ○ simpil
   - ○ simpel
   - ● simple

10. My mother works at the _____ .
    - ○ hospitol
    - ● hospital
    - ○ hospitle

Diagnostic Assessment

Long-Vowel Spelling Patterns

Read each sentence. Fill in the circle next to the long-vowel word that correctly completes the sentence.

1. My mother was _____ to be a computer programmer.
   ○ hird   ○ heired   ○ hired

2. The deer _____ over the small stream.
   ○ leaped   ○ leped   ○ leeped

3. Be sure to _____ all the important ideas in your summary.
   ○ inclood   ○ include   ○ incleud

4. This soup _____ delicious.
   ○ tasts   ○ tastes   ○ taystes

5. The pond was _____ this morning.
   ○ frozen   ○ froazen   ○ froezen

6. We expected _____ people to come to the party.
   ○ fuer   ○ fower   ○ fewer

7. The light _____ was enough to cool us off.
   ○ breeze   ○ breze   ○ breaz

8. You can prevent tooth _____ by brushing regularly.
   ○ decai   ○ decay   ○ decae

9. Which writing _____ do you like?
   ○ style   ○ stile   ○ stail

10. My friend was _____ for the chess team.
    ○ choosen   ○ choasen   ○ chosen

Long-Vowel Spelling Patterns

Read each sentence. Fill in the circle next to the long-vowel word that correctly completes the sentence.

1. My mother was _____ to be a computer programmer.
   ○ hird   ○ heired   ● hired

2. The deer _____ over the small stream.
   ● leaped   ○ leped   ○ leeped

3. Be sure to _____ all the important ideas in your summary.
   ○ inclood   ● include   ○ incleud

4. This soup _____ delicious.
   ○ tasts   ● tastes   ○ taystes

5. The pond was _____ this morning.
   ● frozen   ○ froazen   ○ froezen

6. We expected _____ people to come to the party.
   ○ fuer   ○ fower   ● fewer

7. The light _____ was enough to cool us off.
   ● breeze   ○ breze   ○ breaz

8. You can prevent tooth _____ by brushing regularly.
   ○ decai   ● decay   ○ decae

9. Which writing _____ do you like?
   ● style   ○ stile   ○ stail

10. My friend was _____ for the chess team.
    ○ choosen   ○ choasen   ● chosen

Diagnostic Assessment

Frequently Misspelled Words

Read each sentence. Fill in the circle next to the word that completes the sentence and is spelled correctly.

1. This year, Janie will take her _____ trip to Africa.
   ○ fourth   ○ forth   ○ fourt

2. Collin never puts _____ on his cereal.
   ○ suger   ○ sugar   ○ sugor

3. Kim was _____ to begin the test.
   ○ impatient   ○ impashent   ○ impateint

4. Tory had difficulty writing the third _____ of her news story.
   ○ paragraff   ○ paragraf   ○ paragraph

5. Mitch found a yellowed _____ of paper in an old book.
   ○ peace   ○ piece   ○ peice

6. Mrs. Blankford runs her catering _____ from her own home.
   ○ businez   ○ bizness   ○ business

7. The author of this book makes each _____ come alive.
   ○ charakter   ○ character   ○ karacter

8. Our city zoo just acquired a new _____ .
   ○ giraf   ○ jiraffe   ○ giraffe

9. The ski _____ was snowed in for an entire week.
   ○ lodge   ○ loge   ○ loje

10. The playground was littered with candy _____ .
    ○ wrappers   ○ rappers   ○ wrapers

Frequently Misspelled Words

Read each sentence. Fill in the circle next to the word that completes the sentence and is spelled correctly.

1. This year, Janie will take her _____ trip to Africa.
   - ● fourth
   - ○ forth
   - ○ fourt

2. Collin never puts _____ on his cereal.
   - ○ suger
   - ● sugar
   - ○ sugor

3. Kim was _____ to begin the test.
   - ● impatient
   - ○ impashent
   - ○ impateint

4. Tory had difficulty writing the third _____ of her news story.
   - ○ paragraff
   - ○ paragraf
   - ● paragraph

5. Mitch found a yellowed _____ of paper in an old book.
   - ○ peace
   - ● piece
   - ○ peice

6. Mrs. Blankford runs her catering _____ from her own home.
   - ○ businez
   - ○ bizness
   - ● business

7. The author of this book makes each _____ come alive.
   - ○ charakter
   - ● character
   - ○ karacter

8. Our city zoo just acquired a new _____ .
   - ○ giraf
   - ○ jiraffe
   - ● giraffe

9. The ski _____ was snowed in for an entire week.
   - ● lodge
   - ○ loge
   - ○ loje

10. The playground was littered with candy _____ .
    - ● wrappers
    - ○ rappers
    - ○ wrapers

Vocabulary

The assessments in this section are intended to be completed by a student working independently. The pages for these assessments should be duplicated and distributed to the student. You may find it helpful to read the directions for these assessments out loud before they are administered to ensure that the student understands what to do.

Duplicate the "Student Record" form on page 10 and complete the record for each assessment. You can calculate the percentage correct by hand or look it up in the percentage chart on the inside back cover of this guide. The "Student Record" has space for you to record the observations you make while the student is completing the assessment. Note things such as the speed with which the student works, signs of frustration, attempts at self-correction, and other relevant behaviors.

If some students are having difficulty reading, you may choose to administer the assessments orally. One possibility is to read the assessment to the student and have the student fill in the correct answer. Another possibility is to read the assessment with the student. Allow the student to begin reading, and when the student encounters difficulty, read along with the student until he or she begins reading fluently again.

You may enhance either method of assessment—student reading silently or with your assistance—by asking the student questions like "How do you know that?" or "What makes you sure this answer is right?" The student's answers to these follow-up questions can give you further insight into his or her understanding of the task and his or her ability to read with understanding.

The following chart provides an assessment guideline for each of the fourth-grade Vocabulary assessments.

Assessment	Estimated Percentiles		
	0–49	50–79	80+
Homophones (p. 47)	0–4	5–6	7–8
Content-Area Words (p. 49)	0–5	6–8	9–10
Prefixes, Suffixes, and Root Words (p. 51)	0–5	6–8	9–10
Compound Words (p. 53)	0–5	6–8	9–10
Synonyms and Antonyms (p. 55)	0–5	6–8	9–10
Multiple-Meaning Words (p. 57)	0–3	4–5	6

Homophones

Read each set of sentences. Fill in the circle next to each sentence in which the underlined word is used correctly.

1. ○ The wind <u>blue</u> the kite into the tree.
    ○ The kite was <u>blue</u> with a long, white tail.
    ○ The <u>blew</u> kite was easy to see among the branches.

2. ○ It is <u>to</u> cold in the winter in the Midwest.
    ○ Sometimes I wear <u>too</u> pairs of gloves.
    ○ In <u>two</u> more days it should be warmer.

3. ○ Did you <u>see</u> anything from the roof?
    ○ Could you <u>sea</u> the ocean from that height?
    ○ Wouldn't it be nice to sail on that <u>see</u>?

4. ○ They found <u>there</u> lost cat at home the next day.
    ○ How did she get <u>their</u>?
    ○ <u>They're</u> very relieved to have her back.

5. ○ Which is the <u>right</u> road to take to the beach?
    ○ Did you <u>right</u> down the direction?
    ○ Did you find the <u>write</u> exit ramp?

6. ○ The baker used wheat <u>flower</u> in this bread.
    ○ The singer wore a large, white <u>flower</u> in her hair.
    ○ This is the prettiest <u>flour</u> in the vase.

7. ○ Please don't <u>waist</u> any of that soup.
    ○ The <u>waste</u> size in Don's jeans is 28 inches.
    ○ This belt will fit around Stan's <u>waist</u>.

8. ○ Would you like to <u>buy</u> some oranges?
    ○ The fruit stand is <u>buy</u> the gas station.
    ○ You might want to <u>by</u> some apples, too.

Diagnostic Assessment **47**

Homophones

Read each set of sentences. Fill in the circle next to each sentence in which the underlined word is used correctly.

1. ○ The wind <u>blue</u> the kite into the tree.
   ● The kite was <u>blue</u> with a long, white tail.
   ○ The <u>blew</u> kite was easy to see among the branches.

2. ○ It is <u>to</u> cold in the winter in the Midwest.
   ○ Sometimes I wear <u>too</u> pairs of gloves.
   ● In <u>two</u> more days it should be warmer.

3. ● Did you <u>see</u> anything from the roof?
   ○ Could you <u>sea</u> the ocean from that height?
   ○ Wouldn't it be nice to sail on that <u>see</u>?

4. ○ They found <u>there</u> lost cat at home the next day.
   ○ How did she get <u>their</u>?
   ● <u>They're</u> very relieved to have her back.

5. ● Which is the <u>right</u> road to take to the beach?
   ○ Did you <u>right</u> down the direction?
   ○ Did you find the <u>write</u> exit ramp?

6. ○ The baker used wheat <u>flower</u> in this bread.
   ● The singer wore a large, white <u>flower</u> in her hair.
   ○ This is the prettiest <u>flour</u> in the vase.

7. ○ Please don't <u>waist</u> any of that soup.
   ○ The <u>waste</u> size in Don's jeans is 28 inches.
   ● This belt will fit around Stan's <u>waist</u>.

8. ● Would you like to <u>buy</u> some oranges?
   ○ The fruit stand is <u>buy</u> the gas station.
   ○ You might want to <u>by</u> some apples, too.

Diagnostic Assessment

Content-Area Words

Read each statement. Fill in the circle next to the word that correctly completes the statement.

1. A place where there is little water is a
   ○ slope   ○ desert   ○ lawn

2. Scientists look at stars through a
   ○ telescope   ○ ceiling   ○ forest

3. Addition and subtraction are terms from
   ○ history   ○ health   ○ math

4. A hundred years is called a
   ○ biography   ○ century   ○ history

5. Water that is very hot is
   ○ frozen   ○ shallow   ○ steam

6. Someone who sells things in a store is a
   ○ clerk   ○ customer   ○ student

7. Another name for cows is
   ○ sheep   ○ goats   ○ cattle

8. A low spot between mountains is a
   ○ valley   ○ peak   ○ ridge

9. A kind of energy is
   ○ travel   ○ electricity   ○ responsibility

10. A place that is wet and has lots of plants and animals is a
    ○ swamp   ○ region   ○ suburb

Content-Area Words

Read each statement. Fill in the circle next to the word that correctly completes the statement.

1. A place where there is little water is a
   ○ slope   ● desert   ○ lawn

2. Scientists look at stars through a
   ● telescope   ○ ceiling   ○ forest

3. Addition and subtraction are terms from
   ○ history   ○ health   ● math

4. A hundred years is called a
   ○ biography   ● century   ○ history

5. Water that is very hot is
   ○ frozen   ○ shallow   ● steam

6. Someone who sells things in a store is a
   ● clerk   ○ customer   ○ student

7. Another name for cows is
   ○ sheep   ○ goats   ● cattle

8. A low spot between mountains is a
   ● valley   ○ peak   ○ ridge

9. A kind of energy is
   ○ travel   ● electricity   ○ responsibility

10. A place that is wet and has lots of plants and animals is a
    ● swamp   ○ region   ○ suburb

Diagnostic Assessment

Prefixes, Suffixes, and Root Words

Read each group of words. Fill in the circle next to the
word that has just the <u>prefix</u> underlined.

1. ○ <u>dus</u>ty   ○ <u>dan</u>gerous   ○ <u>dis</u>honor

2. ○ <u>par</u>tial   ○ <u>pre</u>historic   ○ <u>pow</u>dered

3. ○ <u>un</u>button   ○ <u>us</u>ually   ○ <u>ur</u>gent

Read each group of words. Fill in the circle next to the
word that has just the <u>suffix</u> underlined.

4. ○ comfort<u>able</u>   ○ dou<u>ble</u>   ○ fau<u>lty</u>

5. ○ repa<u>ir</u>   ○ inspi<u>re</u>   ○ blend<u>er</u>

6. ○ wint<u>er</u>   ○ violin<u>ist</u>   ○ comf<u>ort</u>

Read each group of words. Fill in the circle next to the
word that has just the <u>root word</u> underlined.

7. ○ cab<u>bage</u>   ○ <u>para</u>chute   ○ <u>guard</u>ian

8. ○ re<u>view</u>   ○ <u>catt</u>le   ○ as<u>cend</u>

9. ○ c<u>atch</u>   ○ <u>tax</u>able   ○ exc<u>ited</u>

10. ○ h<u>edge</u>   ○ un<u>fair</u>ly   ○ pr<u>oblem</u>

Prefixes, Suffixes, and Root Words

Read each group of words. Fill in the circle next to the
word that has just the <u>prefix</u> underlined.

1. ○ <u>dus</u>ty   ○ <u>dan</u>gerous   ● <u>dis</u>honor

2. ○ <u>par</u>tial   ● <u>pre</u>historic   ○ <u>pow</u>dered

3. ● <u>un</u>button   ○ <u>us</u>ually   ○ <u>ur</u>gent

Read each group of words. Fill in the circle next to the
word that has just the <u>suffix</u> underlined.

4. ● comfort<u>able</u> ○ dou<u>ble</u>   ○ faul<u>ty</u>

5. ○ repa<u>ir</u>   ○ inspi<u>re</u>   ● blend<u>er</u>

6. ○ win<u>ter</u>   ● violin<u>ist</u>   ○ comf<u>ort</u>

Read each group of words. Fill in the circle next to the
word that has just the <u>root word</u> underlined.

7. ○ cab<u>bage</u>   ○ <u>para</u>chute   ● <u>guard</u>ian

8. ● re<u>view</u>   ○ <u>cat</u>tle   ○ as<u>cend</u>

9. ○ c<u>atch</u>   ● <u>tax</u>able   ○ ex<u>cited</u>

10. ○ <u>hedge</u>   ● un<u>fair</u>ly   ○ <u>problem</u>

Diagnostic Assessment

Compound Words

**Read each group of words. Fill in the circle next to
the compound word in each group.**

1. ○ merry-go-round   ○ honestly   ○ belonged

2. ○ magazine   ○ newspaper   ○ partners

3. ○ balanced   ○ whispered   ○ everywhere

4. ○ noticing   ○ son-in-law   ○ comfortable

5. ○ emergency   ○ background   ○ geography

6. ○ blast-off   ○ basically   ○ uncovered

7. ○ tornado   ○ lawyer   ○ sunlight

8. ○ paperback   ○ beginning   ○ provide

9. ○ statue   ○ partner   ○ first-rate

10. ○ clearing   ○ anywhere   ○ unlikely

Compound Words

Read each group of words. Fill in the circle next to the compound word in each group.

1. ● merry-go-round ○ honestly ○ belonged

2. ○ magazine ● newspaper ○ partners

3. ○ balanced ○ whispered ● everywhere

4. ○ noticing ● son-in-law ○ comfortable

5. ○ emergency ● background ○ geography

6. ● blast-off ○ basically ○ uncovered

7. ○ tornado ○ lawyer ● sunlight

8. ● paperback ○ beginning ○ provide

9. ○ statue ○ partner ● first-rate

10. ○ clearing ● anywhere ○ unlikely

Diagnostic Assessment

Synonyms and Antonyms

**For Numbers 1 through 5, fill in the circle next to the
synonym for the underlined word in each sentence.**

1. Richard made a <u>silly</u> comment about our friends.
   ○ serious   ○ foolish   ○ thoughtful

2. Sharon has a freckle right in the <u>center</u> of her forehead.
   ○ middle   ○ edge   ○ side

3. The waves <u>destroyed</u> our sand castle.
   ○ repaired   ○ improved   ○ ruined

4. Carla's <u>friend</u> moved to another state.
   ○ stranger   ○ enemy   ○ companion

5. If we <u>join</u> forces, we can succeed more quickly.
   ○ combine   ○ separate   ○ weaken

**Fill in the circle next to the antonym for the underlined
word in each sentence.**

6. Gino said he was <u>sorry</u> about breaking the bowl.
   ○ sad   ○ glad   ○ confused

7. This velvet is very <u>smooth</u> to the touch.
   ○ rough   ○ flat   ○ even

8. The twins usually dress in <u>similar</u> clothing.
   ○ alike   ○ unusual   ○ different

9. Dwayne missed school because he was <u>sick</u>.
   ○ healthy   ○ ill   ○ feverish

10. Barbara was very <u>nervous</u> before getting on stage.
    ○ edgy   ○ calm   ○ jumpy

Synonyms and Antonyms

For Numbers 1 through 5, fill in the circle next to the synonym for the underlined word in each sentence.

1. Richard made a <u>silly</u> comment about our friends.
   - ○ serious
   - ● foolish
   - ○ thoughtful

2. Sharon has a freckle right in the <u>center</u> of her forehead.
   - ● middle
   - ○ edge
   - ○ side

3. The waves <u>destroyed</u> our sand castle.
   - ○ repaired
   - ○ improved
   - ● ruined

4. Carla's <u>friend</u> moved to another state.
   - ○ stranger
   - ○ enemy
   - ● companion

5. If we <u>join</u> forces, we can succeed more quickly.
   - ● combine
   - ○ separate
   - ○ weaken

Fill in the circle next to the antonym for the underlined word in each sentence.

6. Gino said he was <u>sorry</u> about breaking the bowl.
   - ○ sad
   - ● glad
   - ○ confused

7. This velvet is very <u>smooth</u> to the touch.
   - ● rough
   - ○ flat
   - ○ even

8. The twins usually dress in <u>similar</u> clothing.
   - ○ alike
   - ○ unusual
   - ● different

9. Dwayne missed school because he was <u>sick</u>.
   - ● healthy
   - ○ ill
   - ○ feverish

10. Barbara was very <u>nervous</u> before getting on stage.
    - ○ edgy
    - ● calm
    - ○ jumpy

Diagnostic Assessment

Multiple-Meaning Words

Read each question. Fill in the circle next to the answer you think is correct.

1. In which sentence does the word <u>hold</u> mean "part of a ship"?
   - ○ How long can you <u>hold</u> your breath?
   - ○ <u>Hold</u> this box for me, please.
   - ○ The <u>hold</u> was filled with cars bound for America.

2. In which sentence does the word <u>check</u> mean "look over"?
   - ○ Put a <u>check</u> beside each book you have read.
   - ○ Before you turn your test in, <u>check</u> your work.
   - ○ This <u>check</u> is for ten dollars.

3. In which sentence does the word <u>pass</u> mean "an opening in the mountains"?
   - ○ Henry threw a <u>pass</u> to Martin, but he just missed it.
   - ○ Shannon was able to <u>pass</u> the other runners on the hill.
   - ○ The travelers were looking for the <u>pass</u> that would lead to Oregon.

4. In which sentence does the word <u>roll</u> mean "something you eat"?
   - ○ Put a <u>roll</u> on each plate.
   - ○ The <u>roll</u> of stamps is in the drawer.
   - ○ Let's <u>roll</u> the log over and see what's under it.

5. In which sentence does the word <u>snap</u> mean "easy"?
   - ○ Running a mile is a <u>snap</u> for Christie.
   - ○ The dog will come if you <u>snap</u> your fingers.
   - ○ We heard a twig <u>snap</u> behind us.

6. In which sentence does the word <u>rest</u> mean "a portion of"?
   - ○ We can <u>rest</u> when we reach the end of this trail.
   - ○ When will you finish reading the <u>rest</u> of the book?
   - ○ The baby is taking a <u>rest</u> now.

Multiple-Meaning Words

Read each question. Fill in the circle next to the
answer you think is correct.

1. In which sentence does the word <u>hold</u> mean "part of a ship"?
   - ○ How long can you <u>hold</u> your breath?
   - ○ <u>Hold</u> this box for me, please.
   - ● The <u>hold</u> was filled with cars bound for America.

2. In which sentence does the word <u>check</u> mean "look over"?
   - ○ Put a <u>check</u> beside each book you have read.
   - ● Before you turn your test in, <u>check</u> your work.
   - ○ This <u>check</u> is for ten dollars.

3. In which sentence does the word <u>pass</u> mean "an opening
   in the mountains"?
   - ○ Henry threw a <u>pass</u> to Martin, but he just missed it.
   - ○ Shannon was able to <u>pass</u> the other runners on the hill.
   - ● The travelers were looking for the <u>pass</u> that would lead to Oregon.

4. In which sentence does the word <u>roll</u> mean "something you eat"?
   - ● Put a <u>roll</u> on each plate.
   - ○ The <u>roll</u> of stamps is in the drawer.
   - ○ Let's <u>roll</u> the log over and see what's under it.

5. In which sentence does the word <u>snap</u> mean "easy"?
   - ● Running a mile is a <u>snap</u> for Christie.
   - ○ The dog will come if you <u>snap</u> your fingers.
   - ○ We heard a twig <u>snap</u> behind us.

6. In which sentence does the word <u>rest</u> mean "a portion of"?
   - ○ We can <u>rest</u> when we reach the end of this trail.
   - ● When will you finish reading the <u>rest</u> of the book?
   - ○ The baby is taking a <u>rest</u> now.

Diagnostic Assessment

Silent Reading Comprehension

Silent Reading Comprehension

The assessments in this section are intended to be completed by a student working independently. The pages for these assessments should be duplicated and distributed to the student. You may find it helpful to read the directions for these assessments out loud before they are administered to ensure that the student understands what to do.

Duplicate the "Student Record" form on page 10 and complete the record for each assessment. You can calculate the percentage correct by hand or look it up in the percentage chart on the inside back cover of this guide. The "Student Record" has space for you to record the observations you make while the student is completing the assessment. Note things such as the speed with which the student works, signs of frustration, attempts at self-correction, and other relevant behaviors.

If some students are having difficulty reading, you may choose to administer the assessments orally. One possibility is to read the assessment to the student and have the student fill in the correct answer. Another possibility is to read the assessment with the student. Allow the student to begin reading, and when the student encounters difficulty, read along with the student until he or she begins reading fluently again.

You may enhance either method of assessment—student reading silently or with your assistance—by asking the student questions like "How do you know that?" or "What makes you sure this answer is right?" The student's answers to these follow-up questions can give you further insight into his or her understanding of the task and his or her ability to read with understanding.

The following chart provides an assessment guideline for each of the fourth-grade Silent Reading Comprehension assessments.

Assessment	Estimated Percentiles		
	0–49	50–79	80+
Plot, Character, Conflict, and Setting (p. 61)	0–1	2–3	4
Sequence (p. 63)	0–2	3–4	5
Cause and Effect (p. 65)	0–1	2–3	4
Author's Purpose (p. 67)	0–3	4–5	6
Persuasive Writing (p. 69)	0–1	2–3	4
Describe a Process (p. 71)	0–1	2–3	4

Plot, Character, Conflict, and Setting

**Read each passage. Fill in the circle next to the
best answer to each question.**

Prince Richard brought his horse to a stop. He listened
carefully and looked into the dark forest on both sides of the
road. Suddenly, a dozen soldiers ran from behind the trees.
Before he could do anything, they had grabbed the reins of his
horse. He saw no possibility of escape.

1. What is the plot of this story?
   - ○ a road in a dark forest
   - ○ a time long ago
   - ○ the capture of the prince

2. Who is the main character in this story?
   - ○ Prince Richard
   - ○ the horses
   - ○ the soldiers

The children stood on their skis at the top of the hill.
When the instructor waved, they skied toward him one at a
time. Even though it was an easy slope, Susan was a little
afraid. She had never been on skis before. She took a deep
breath, pushed off with her poles, and headed down the slope.

3. The conflict of this story is
   - ○ a ski resort in the Rockies.
   - ○ winter vacation last year.
   - ○ Susan confronting her fear of being on skis.

4. Where did the author establish the setting for the story?
   - ○ on a park trail
   - ○ on an easy ski slope
   - ○ at a summer resort

Diagnostic Assessment **61**

Plot, Character, Conflict, and Setting

Read each passage. Fill in the circle next to the best answer to each question.

Prince Richard brought his horse to a stop. He listened carefully and looked into the dark forest on both sides of the road. Suddenly, a dozen soldiers ran from behind the trees. Before he could do anything, they had grabbed the reins of his horse. He saw no possibility of escape.

1. What is the plot of this story?
- ○ a road in a dark forest
- ○ a time long ago
- ● the capture of the prince

2. Who is the main character in this story?
- ● Prince Richard
- ○ the horses
- ○ the soldiers

The children stood on their skis at the top of the hill. When the instructor waved, they skied toward him one at a time. Even though it was an easy slope, Susan was a little afraid. She had never been on skis before. She took a deep breath, pushed off with her poles, and headed down the slope.

3. The conflict of this story is
- ○ a ski resort in the Rockies.
- ○ winter vacation last year.
- ● Susan confronting her fear of being on skis.

4. Where did the author establish the setting for the story?
- ○ on a park trail
- ● on an easy ski slope
- ○ at a summer resort

Diagnostic Assessment

Sequence

Read the paragraph. Fill in the circle next to the correct answer to each question.

The first thing Yolanda did was prepare the soil by tilling it and getting rid of rocks and old roots. Next, she added compost and mixed it in thoroughly. When the soil was ready, she planted the flower seeds, following the directions on the package. She put the seeds about three inches apart, so that the garden wouldn't be too crowded. For the next few days, she kept the soil moist. Finally, after just a few days, green shoots poked through the soil.

1. Yolanda **began** by
   ○ planting the seeds.   ○ adding compost to the soil.
   ○ keeping the soil moist.   ○ preparing the soil.

2. What did she do **after** adding compost?
   ○ She got rid of rocks and old roots.   ○ She prepared the soil.
   ○ She mixed it in thoroughly.   ○ She tilled the soil.

3. What happened **last**?
   ○ The flowers started growing.   ○ Yolanda planted seeds.
   ○ Yolanda added compost.   ○ The seeds were soaked in water.

4. What did Yolanda do **after** planting the seeds?
   ○ She got rid of rocks and old roots.   ○ She read the seed packages.
   ○ She added compost to the soil.   ○ She kept the soil moist.

5. Which sequence of words are used in this paragraph?
   ○ first, next, and finally   ○ prepare, ready, and following
   ○ getting, added, and mixed   ○ when, so, and for

Sequence

Read the paragraph. Fill in the circle next to the correct answer to each question.

The first thing Yolanda did was prepare the soil by tilling it and getting rid of rocks and old roots. Next, she added compost and mixed it in thoroughly. When the soil was ready, she planted the flower seeds, following the directions on the package. She put the seeds about three inches apart, so that the garden wouldn't be too crowded. For the next few days, she kept the soil moist. Finally, after just a few days, green shoots poked through the soil.

1. Yolanda **began** by
   ○ planting the seeds.   ○ adding compost to the soil.
   ○ keeping the soil moist.   ● preparing the soil.

2. What did she do **after** adding compost?
   ○ She got rid of rocks and old roots.   ○ She prepared the soil.
   ● She mixed it in thoroughly.   ○ She tilled the soil.

3. What happened **last**?
   ● The flowers started growing.   ○ Yolanda planted seeds.
   ○ Yolanda added compost.   ○ The seeds were soaked in water.

4. What did Yolanda do **after** planting the seeds?
   ○ She got rid of rocks and old roots.   ○ She read the seed packages.
   ○ She added compost to the soil.   ● She kept the soil moist.

5. Which sequence of words are used in this paragraph?
   ● first, next, and finally   ○ prepare, ready, and following
   ○ getting, added, and mixed   ○ when, so, and for

Diagnostic Assessment

Cause and Effect

Read the story and the questions. Fill in the circle next to the best answer to each question.

Tina heard the rain start to fall and rushed to close the windows. Just then, the wind picked up, lightning hit a power line, and the electricity went off. Tina knew exactly what to do. She started for the kitchen to get some candles and a flashlight. On the way, she bumped her knee because she couldn't see well in the dark. After she reached the kitchen and found the flashlight, everything was easier. Tina thought it was fun to be without lights. Then she remembered her homework and wasn't happy. She wouldn't be able to finish it because the computer needed electricity.

1. What caused the electricity to go off?
- ○ The rain flooded the power station.
- ○ Lightning hit a power line.
- ○ The wind blew a pole down.

2. Which of these is an effect of the falling rain?
- ○ Tina rushed to close the windows.
- ○ The wind picked up.
- ○ The windows were open.

3. Why did Tina bump her knee?
- ○ She was rushing into the kitchen.
- ○ She was thinking about her homework.
- ○ She couldn't see because there were no lights.

4. What caused Tina to be unhappy?
- ○ remembering that she had misplaced her homework
- ○ remembering that she had bumped her knee
- ○ remembering that the computer needed electricity

Diagnostic Assessment **65**

Cause and Effect

Read the story and the questions. Fill in the circle next
to the best answer to each question.

Tina heard the rain start to fall and rushed to close the
windows. Just then, the wind picked up, lightning hit a power
line, and the electricity went off. Tina knew exactly what to
do. She started for the kitchen to get some candles and a
flashlight. On the way, she bumped her knee because she
couldn't see well in the dark. After she reached the kitchen
and found the flashlight, everything was easier. Tina thought
it was fun to be without lights. Then she remembered her
homework and wasn't happy. She wouldn't be able to finish it
because the computer needed electricity.

1. What caused the electricity to go off?
   ○ The rain flooded the power station.
   ● Lightning hit a power line.
   ○ The wind blew a pole down.

2. Which of these is an effect of the falling rain?
   ● Tina rushed to close the windows.
   ○ The wind picked up.
   ○ The windows were open.

3. Why did Tina bump her knee?
   ○ She was rushing into the kitchen.
   ○ She was thinking about her homework.
   ● She couldn't see because there were no lights.

4. What caused Tina to be unhappy?
   ○ remembering that she had misplaced her homework
   ○ remembering that she had bumped her knee
   ● remembering that the computer needed electricity

Diagnostic Assessment

Author's Purpose

Read each paragraph. Fill in the circle next to the reason why the author wrote the paragraph.

1. Lettuce is a tasty food that is available all year. Most supermarkets carry several kinds of lettuce, including iceberg and romaine.
   ○ inform   ○ entertain   ○ persuade   ○ explain

2. The pilot circled the lake and then landed the plane in a quiet cove. It drifted on its pontoons into the shore and came to a gentle stop. She and the other passengers jumped out and began unloading their camping gear.
   ○ inform   ○ entertain   ○ persuade   ○ explain

3. Remove the old faucet carefully. Place the rubber gasket over the holes in the sink, then put the new faucet on top. Gently press it down, then fasten the nuts that will hold it in place.
   ○ inform   ○ entertain   ○ persuade   ○ explain

4. The teaching award should go to Ms. Jackson. Even though this is her first year at Rio Rancho High School, she's done a great job. She has made us love foreign languages and encouraged us to do our best in other subjects.
   ○ inform   ○ entertain   ○ persuade   ○ explain

5. Pizza is a popular food that started out as a way to use leftovers. When people baked bread, they sometimes had small pieces of dough left over. They would flatten this dough and cover it with tomatoes, cheese, and spices.
   ○ inform   ○ entertain   ○ persuade   ○ explain

6. Pour all the ingredients into a medium pot. Stir in two cups of water and bring to a boil. Cook on medium heat for five minutes. Remove the pot from the burner and let stand for five minutes before serving.
   ○ inform   ○ entertain   ○ persuade   ○ explain

Author's Purpose

Read each paragraph. Fill in the circle next to the
reason why the author wrote the paragraph.

1. Lettuce is a tasty food that is available all year. Most
   supermarkets carry several kinds of lettuce, including iceberg
   and romaine.

   ● inform   ○ entertain   ○ persuade   ○ explain

2. The pilot circled the lake and then landed the plane in a quiet
   cove. It drifted on its pontoons into the shore and came to a
   gentle stop. She and the other passengers jumped out and
   began unloading their camping gear.

   ○ inform   ● entertain   ○ persuade   ○ explain

3. Remove the old faucet carefully. Place the rubber gasket over
   the holes in the sink, then put the new faucet on top. Gently
   press it down, then fasten the nuts that will hold it in place.

   ○ inform   ○ entertain   ○ persuade   ● explain

4. The teaching award should go to Ms. Jackson. Even though
   this is her first year at Rio Rancho High School, she's done
   a great job. She has made us love foreign languages and
   encouraged us to do our best in other subjects.

   ○ inform   ○ entertain   ● persuade   ○ explain

5. Pizza is a popular food that started out as a way to use
   leftovers. When people baked bread, they sometimes had
   small pieces of dough left over. They would flatten this dough
   and cover it with tomatoes, cheese, and spices.

   ● inform   ○ entertain   ○ persuade   ○ explain

6. Pour all the ingredients into a medium pot. Stir in two cups
   of water and bring to a boil. Cook on medium heat for five
   minutes. Remove the pot from the burner and let stand for
   five minutes before serving.

   ○ inform   ○ entertain   ○ persuade   ● explain

Diagnostic Assessment

Persuasive Writing

Read each passage and the questions that follow it. Fill in the circle next to the correct answer to each question.

Andy's parents were having a garage sale. They told him he could keep the money from the sale of any of his own things. So Andy advertised his items on the following sign:
"Like sports? Try these great track shoes.
Everyone needs music. Check out the latest CDs.
Are you bored? Play a video game!
Want to look good? Try on some stone-washed jeans."

1. What was the purpose of Andy's sign?
   ○ to convince people to buy his things
   ○ to show people that he had many things
   ○ to help his parents buy more things

2. What did Andy do to make his sign persuade people?
   ○ He talked about the quality of his things.
   ○ He supported his arguments with facts.
   ○ He tried to appeal to people's interests.

If you want to earn money, you should start your own business. You can make more money from your own business than from an after-school job because your business can expand. You can hire people to work for you. Then, you can collect money for the work that other people do. After you pay your workers, you will still have money that you didn't have to spend time earning.

3. What is the purpose of this passage?
   ○ to urge people to start a business
   ○ to convince people to work for others
   ○ to talk people into hiring more workers

4. What did the writer do to persuade people?
   ○ The writer supported arguments with facts.
   ○ The writer supported arguments with reasons.
   ○ The writer appealed to people's feelings.

Persuasive Writing

Read each passage and the questions that follow it. Fill in the circle next to the correct answer to each question.

Andy's parents were having a garage sale. They told him he could keep the money from the sale of any of his own things. So Andy advertised his items on the following sign:
"Like sports? Try these great track shoes.
Everyone needs music. Check out the latest CDs.
Are you bored? Play a video game!
Want to look good? Try on some stone-washed jeans."

1. What was the purpose of Andy's sign?
- ⬤ to convince people to buy his things
- ○ to show people that he had many things
- ○ to help his parents buy more things

2. What did Andy do to make his sign persuade people?
- ○ He talked about the quality of his things.
- ○ He supported his arguments with facts.
- ⬤ He tried to appeal to people's interests.

If you want to earn money, you should start your own business. You can make more money from your own business than from an after-school job because your business can expand. You can hire people to work for you. Then, you can collect money for the work that other people do. After you pay your workers, you will still have money that you didn't have to spend time earning.

3. What is the purpose of this passage?
- ⬤ to urge people to start a business
- ○ to convince people to work for others
- ○ to talk people into hiring more workers

4. What did the writer do to persuade people?
- ○ The writer supported arguments with facts.
- ⬤ The writer supported arguments with reasons.
- ○ The writer appealed to people's feelings.

Describe a Process

Read the information in the box. Fill in the circle next to the correct answer to each question.

Steps to Follow in Case of a Fire

- In a single file, walk quickly out of the building.
- Respond to the fire alarm when you hear it.
- Stand outside with your class until a school official tells you to go back inside.
- File out of the room in an orderly way.
- Stand up next to your desk.

---

1. Which step should come first?
   - ○ File out of the room in an orderly way.
   - ○ Respond to the fire alarm when you hear it.
   - ○ Stand up next to your desk.

2. Which step should come second?
   - ○ Do not ignore the fire alarm.
   - ○ Stand outside with your class until a school official tells you to go back inside.
   - ○ Stand up next to your desk.

3. Which step should come third?
   - ○ File out of the room in an orderly way.
   - ○ Stand outside with your class until a school official tells you to go back inside.
   - ○ In a single file, walk quickly out of the building.

4. Which step should come fourth?
   - ○ File out of the room in an orderly way.
   - ○ In a single file, walk quickly out of the building.
   - ○ Stand up next to your desk.

Describe a Process

Read the information in the box. Fill in the circle next
to the correct answer to each question.

Steps to Follow in Case of a Fire

- In a single file, walk quickly out of the building.
- Respond to the fire alarm when you hear it.
- Stand outside with your class until a school official
  tells you to go back inside.
- File out of the room in an orderly way.
- Stand up next to your desk.

---

1. Which step should come first?
- ○ File out of the room in an orderly way.
- ● Respond to the fire alarm when you hear it.
- ○ Stand up next to your desk.

2. Which step should come second?
- ○ Do not ignore the fire alarm.
- ○ Stand outside with your class until a school official tells you
  to go back inside.
- ● Stand up next to your desk.

3. Which step should come third?
- ● File out of the room in an orderly way.
- ○ Stand outside with your class until a school official tells you
  to go back inside.
- ○ In a single file, walk quickly out of the building.

4. Which step should come fourth?
- ○ File out of the room in an orderly way.
- ● In a single file, walk quickly out of the building.
- ○ Stand up next to your desk.

Diagnostic Assessment

Oral Word Reading
Oral Fluency Assessment

Oral Word Reading

Specific instructions for administration are included with each Oral Word Reading assessment. Duplicate the "Student Record" page and give it to the student. Duplicate the scoring page for your use to record each student's scores and any observations.

For instructions on scoring and interpreting these assessments, see Oral Word Reading Introduction.

Oral Fluency Assessment

These directions will help you administer the Oral Fluency Assessments for fifth-grade students. Reproduce the "Student Prompt" page once and save it for use with multiple students. Reproduce the "Student Record" page for each student receiving the assessment. Fill in the name and date information. Give the "Student Prompt" to the student with the following directions:

Say: Here is a story I would like you to read out loud for me. I am going to listen to you read and take some notes. The notes I take will help me learn how well you can read. You will not be graded for this, so you should not feel nervous. Read the story carefully and do your best. Take a few minutes now to look over the story, and then I will tell you when to begin.

Allow time for the student to preview the story. Be sure you have a pen or pencil, the "Student Record," a stopwatch or other timer, and any other materials you may need.

Say: Are you ready? You may begin now.

Start the timer or watch as the student begins to read. You may pronounce any proper nouns with which the student is unfamiliar. Do not count these words as errors

As the student reads, draw a line through each word the student misreads. If possible, note each type of error the student makes by writing it on the "Student Record."

For specific instructions on scoring and interpreting these assessments, see Oral Fluency Introduction.

Oral Word Reading: Student Record
Fifth Grade (Beginning of year)

Name _____ Date _____

here	than	now	only	just
same	every	find	house	school
number	night	money	heard	power
believe	interest	nearly	beautiful	action

Directions

Duplicate page 76 and give it to the student. Duplicate this page and use it as a Student Record for scoring and noting your observations.

Say: Here are some words I would like you to read for me. Read each row of words. If you are not sure how to read a word, take your best guess. You may begin now.

As the student reads, circle each word the student reads wrong. If possible, note the type of error, for example, reading *made* as *mad*. Also, observe the student as she or he reads and record any relevant observations in the space below.

Fifth Grade (Beginning of year)

20 Words   **Number Correct** _____   **Percent Correct** _____

(Multiply the number of correct words by 5 to find the percent correct.)

Observations

_____

_____

_____

_____

_____

_____

Oral Word Reading: Student Prompt

here	than	now	only	just
same	every	find	house	school
number	night	money	heard	power
believe	interest	nearly	beautiful	action

Diagnostic Assessment

Oral Word Reading: Student Record
Fifth Grade (Middle of year)

Name _____ Date _____

mother	course	whole	behind	anything
ground	probably	toward	among	picture
himself	person	miles	already	remember
tried	common	amount	special	tree

Directions

Duplicate page 78 and give it to the student. Duplicate this page and use it as a Student Record for scoring and noting your observations.

Say: Here are some words I would like you to read for me. Read each row of words. If you are not sure how to read a word, take your best guess. You may begin now.

As the student reads, circle each word the student reads wrong. If possible, note the type of error, for example, reading *made* as *mad*. Also, observe the student as she or he reads and record any relevant observations in the space below.

Fifth Grade (Middle of year)

20 Words   **Number Correct** _____   **Percent Correct** _____

(Multiply the number of correct words by 5 to find the percent correct.)

Observations

_____

_____

_____

_____

_____

_____

Oral Word Reading: Student Prompt

mother	course	whole	behind	anything
ground	probably	toward	among	picture
himself	person	miles	already	remember
tried	common	amount	special	tree

Diagnostic Assessment

Oral Word Reading: Student Record
Fifth Grade (End of year)

Name _____ Date _____

learned	morning	ago	seemed	everything
quite	whether	higher	round	easily
suppose	nature	helped	century	larger
company	energy	brought	whose	direction

Directions

Duplicate page 80 and give it to the student. Duplicate this page and use it as a Student Record for scoring and noting your observations.

Say: Here are some words I would like you to read for me. Read each row of words. If you are not sure how to read a word, take your best guess. You may begin now.

As the student reads, circle each word the student reads wrong. If possible, note the type of error, for example, reading *made* as *mad*. Also, observe the student as she or he reads and record any relevant observations in the space below.

Fifth Grade (End of year)

20 Words   **Number Correct** _____   **Percent Correct** _____

(Multiply the number of correct words by 5 to find the percent correct.)

Observations

_____

_____

_____

_____

_____

_____

Oral Word Reading: Student Prompt

learned	morning	ago	seemed	everything
quite	whether	higher	round	easily
suppose	nature	helped	century	larger
company	energy	brought	whose	direction

Diagnostic Assessment

Oral Fluency Assessment: Student Record
Fifth Grade (Beginning of year)

Name _____   Date _____

Building a Country

One of the best examples of cooperation in history is the United States. The United States was born more than two hundred years ago. It happened because people were willing to cooperate. It survives today for the same reason.

Long ago, America was controlled by European countries. One of these countries was England. The people in America decided to band together and form a new country that was independent. The people living in America had come from many different places and had different interests. Even so, they joined forces and fought a war for independence from England. They won the war, but now they faced an even greater task—building a new country.

After the war, the people formed a new government that depended on cooperation. People in each state would vote for officials such as a president, a governor, and senators. Whoever got the most votes would win the election. The people who voted had to cooperate and support the officials who were elected. This kind of cooperation was unusual at that time, but it worked.

The biggest challenge to the United States came during the Civil War. The states in the South wanted to leave the United States. The states in the North didn't want this. They fought a war that the North won. After the war, the people once more cooperated, and the country was united again. Since that time, people have had different opinions. They still cooperate with one another, however, and today America is a wonderful place to live.

1–14
15–27
28–39
40–50
51–62
63–74
75–86
87–98
99–113
114–125
126–138
139–151
152–164
165–177
178–189
190–203
204–217
218–229
230–240
241–251
252–254

EVALUATING CODES FOR ORAL FLUENCY

sky (/) words read incorrectly

blue
^ sky (^) inserted word
( ]) after the last word

READING RATE AND ACCURACY

Total Words Read: _____

Number of Errors: – _____

Number of Correct Words Read Per Minute (WPM): _____

Accuracy Rate: _____

READING FLUENCY

	Low	Average	High
Decoding ability	○	○	○
Pace	○	○	○
Syntax	○	○	○
Self-correction	○	○	○
Intonation	○	○	○

Oral Fluency Assessment: Student Prompt

Building a Country

One of the best examples of cooperation in history is the United States. The United States was born more than two hundred years ago. It happened because people were willing to cooperate. It survives today for the same reason.

Long ago, America was controlled by European countries. One of these countries was England. The people in America decided to band together and form a new country that was independent. The people living in America had come from many different places and had different interests. Even so, they joined forces and fought a war for independence from England. They won the war, but now they faced an even greater task—building a new country.

After the war, the people formed a new government that depended on cooperation. People in each state would vote for officials such as a president, a governor, and senators. Whoever got the most votes would win the election. The people who voted had to cooperate and support the officials who were elected. This kind of cooperation was unusual at that time, but it worked.

The biggest challenge to the United States came during the Civil War. The states in the South wanted to leave the United States. The states in the North didn't want this. They fought a war that the North won. After the war, the people once more cooperated, and the country was united again. Since that time, people have had different opinions. They still cooperate with one another, however, and today America is a wonderful place to live.

Diagnostic Assessment

Oral Fluency Assessment: Student Record
Fifth Grade (Middle of year)

Name _____ **Date** _____

The Trunk

In the corner of the Jackson's living room is a small trunk. Most of the
time, no one pays much attention to it. Sometimes the cat sits on it, and
Mrs. Jackson often puts flowers on it. Other than that, the trunk just sits
in the corner.

During the holidays, however, the trunk becomes very important. When
everyone comes to visit, they want to look at family pictures. These pictures
are stored in the trunk, so in a way, it is a treasure chest of memories.

Here is what normally happens. Grandfather Jackson sits on the sofa. One
of the grandchildren pushes the trunk over to him. Grandfather
slowly opens the lid of the trunk and reaches inside. He pulls out some
pictures and says, "Let's see what we have here. Can one of you children
help me? I'm not sure who is in this picture?" He is only kidding when he
says this. He knows exactly who is in every picture.

The children take turns talking about the pictures. They explain who is
in each picture and where it was taken. Sometimes they forget details about
a picture, so Grandfather will help them out. Everyone has a wonderful
time because the pictures bring back such good memories.

Some of the pictures are very special. These are pictures from many years
ago. They show family members the children have never met because they
lived so long ago. Grandfather was just a little boy when some of the
pictures were taken, but he remembers the stories as if they were taken
just yesterday.

1–15	
16–30	
31–44	
45–47	
48–57	
58–70	
71–86	
87–98	
99–108	
109–122	
123–136	
137–152	
153–162	
163–174	
175–187	
188–199	
200–208	
209–221	
222–233	
234–247	
248–260	
261–262	

EVALUATING CODES FOR ORAL FLUENCY

sky   (/) words read incorrectly

blue
^   sky   (^) inserted word
           ( ]) after the last word

READING RATE AND ACCURACY

Total Words Read: _____

Number of Errors: − _____

Number of Correct Words
Read Per Minute (WPM):   _____

Accuracy Rate: _____

READING FLUENCY

	Low	Average	High
Decoding ability	O	O	O
Pace	O	O	O
Syntax	O	O	O
Self-correction	O	O	O
Intonation	O	O	O

The Trunk

In the corner of the Jackson's living room is a small trunk. Most of the time, no one pays much attention to it. Sometimes the cat sits on it, and Mrs. Jackson often puts flowers on it. Other than that, the trunk just sits in the corner.

During the holidays, however, the trunk becomes very important. When everyone comes to visit, they want to look at family pictures. These pictures are stored in the trunk, so in a way, it is a treasure chest of memories.

Here is what normally happens. Grandfather Jackson sits on the sofa. One of the grandchildren pushes the trunk over to him. Grandfather slowly opens the lid of the trunk and reaches inside. He pulls out some pictures and says, "Let's see what we have here. Can one of you children help me? I'm not sure who is in this picture?" He is only kidding when he says this. He knows exactly who is in every picture.

The children take turns talking about the pictures. They explain who is in each picture and where it was taken. Sometimes they forget details about a picture, so Grandfather will help them out. Everyone has a wonderful time because the pictures bring back such good memories.

Some of the pictures are very special. These are pictures from many years ago. They show family members the children have never met because they lived so long ago. Grandfather was just a little boy when some of the pictures were taken, but he remembers the stories as if they were taken just yesterday.

 Diagnostic Assessment

Oral Fluency Assessment: Student Record
Fifth Grade (End of year)

Name _____ **Date** _____

The Highest Hike

Luke put his arms through the straps of his backpack. His sister,	1–12
Kate, made sure the pack was closed and all the straps were tight.	13–25
Luke then did the same for her. They were ready to go.	26–37
"Are you kids ready?" asked Uncle Al. "We should get started now	38–49
while it's cool. I'd like to make the top of that ridge by lunchtime."	50–63
He pointed to a spot about halfway up the mountain.	64–73
"Yep," answered Kate. "We've left nothing behind, and the fire is out.	74–85
This was a great spot to camp, Uncle Al."	86–94
"How high is the ridge," asked Luke, "and how much higher is the	95–107
top of the mountain?"	108–111
"The ridge is about 10,000 feet. When we get there, we'll have lunch	112–124
and rest for a while. This afternoon, we'll hike from the ridge to just about	125–139
the top of the mountain. There's a great spot to camp there. Then	140–152
tomorrow morning, we'll go all the way up. The top of the mountain	153–165
is over 14,000 feet."	166–169
"That will be our highest hike ever," said Kate. "Will it be much	170–182
different from the other hikes we've gone on out West?"	183–192
"A little," answered Uncle Al. "You'll notice that it will be a little	193–205
harder to breathe. The higher you go, the less oxygen there is. And	206–218
toward the top, there won't be any trees at all. On all our other hikes,	219–233
we've been in forests all the way to the top of the mountain. Well, let's	234–248
get started. We have about eight miles to go before we reach that ridge."	249–262

**EVALUATING CODES
FOR ORAL FLUENCY**

sky   (/) words read incorrectly

blue

^   sky   (^) inserted word

            ( ]) after the last word

READING RATE AND ACCURACY

Total Words Read: _____

Number of Errors: – _____

Number of Correct Words
Read Per Minute (WPM):   _____

Accuracy Rate: _____

READING FLUENCY

	Low	Average	High
Decoding ability	○	○	○
Pace	○	○	○
Syntax	○	○	○
Self-correction	○	○	○
Intonation	○	○	○

The Highest Hike

Luke put his arms through the straps of his backpack. His sister, Kate, made sure the pack was closed and all the straps were tight. Luke then did the same for her. They were ready to go.

"Are you kids ready?" asked Uncle Al. "We should get started now while it's cool. I'd like to make the top of that ridge by lunchtime." He pointed to a spot about halfway up the mountain.

"Yep," answered Kate. "We've left nothing behind, and the fire is out. This was a great spot to camp, Uncle Al."

"How high is the ridge," asked Luke, "and how much higher is the top of the mountain?"

"The ridge is about 10,000 feet. When we get there, we'll have lunch and rest for a while. This afternoon, we'll hike from the ridge to just about the top of the mountain. There's a great spot to camp there. Then tomorrow morning, we'll go all the way up. The top of the mountain is over 14,000 feet."

"That will be our highest hike ever," said Kate. "Will it be much different from the other hikes we've gone on out West?"

"A little," answered Uncle Al. "You'll notice that it will be a little harder to breathe. The higher you go, the less oxygen there is. And toward the top, there won't be any trees at all. On all our other hikes, we've been in forests all the way to the top of the mountain. Well, let's get started. We have about eight miles to go before we reach that ridge."

 Diagnostic Assessment

Fifth Grade
Spelling

Spelling

The assessments in this section are intended to be completed by a student working independently. The pages for these assessments should be duplicated and distributed to the student. You may find it helpful to read the directions for these assessments out loud before they are administered to ensure that the student understands what to do.

Duplicate the "Student Record" form on page 10 and complete the record for each assessment. You can calculate the percentage correct by hand or look it up in the percentage chart on the inside back cover of this guide. The "Student Record" has space for you to record the observations you make while the student is completing the assessment. Note things such as the speed with which the student works, signs of frustration, attempts at self-correction, and other relevant behaviors.

If some students are having difficulty reading, you may choose to administer the assessments orally. One possibility is to read the assessment to the student and have the student fill in the correct answer. Another possibility is to read the assessment with the student. Allow the student to begin reading, and when the student encounters difficulty, read along with the student until he or she begins reading fluently again.

You may enhance either method of assessment—student reading silently or with your assistance—by asking the student questions like "How do you know that?" or "What makes you sure this answer is right?" The student's answers to these follow-up questions can give you further insight into his or her understanding of the task and his or her ability to read with understanding.

The following chart provides an assessment guideline for each of the fifth-grade Spelling assessments.

Assessment	Estimated Percentiles		
	0–49	50–79	80+
Different Spellings for the /er/ Sound (p. 89)	0–5	6–8	9–10
Consonant Before -le Spelling Pattern (p. 91)	0–5	6–8	9–10
Frequently Misspelled Words (p. 93)	0–5	6–8	9–10
Consonant Blends and Digraphs (p. 95)	0–5	6–8	9–10
Homophones (p. 97)	0–3	4–5	6–7
Long-Vowel Spellings (p. 99)	0–5	6–8	9–10

Name _____ Date _____

Different Spellings for the /er/ Sound

Read each sentence. Fill in the circle next to the word that correctly completes the sentence.

1. The settlers _____ their first winter in the new land.
   ○ survived   ○ servived   ○ sirvived

2. The students learned to _____ a computer.
   ○ opirate   ○ opurate   ○ operate

3. The road curved _____ over the mountain.
   ○ upword   ○ upward   ○ upwird

4. Birds _____ as the sun came up.
   ○ chirped   ○ cherped   ○ churped

5. One of my favorite subjects is _____.
   ○ histery   ○ histury   ○ history

6. Lottie holds the school _____ for running a mile.
   ○ recird   ○ record   ○ recurd

7. This is the most _____ way to get to the swimming pool.
   ○ durect   ○ darect   ○ direct

8. It was a _____ day for a baseball game.
   ○ perfict   ○ purfect   ○ perfect

9. Everything in this store costs less than a _____ .
   ○ dollar   ○ doller   ○ dollir

10. People _____ to their cars as soon as it started raining.
    ○ herried   ○ hurried   ○ hirried

Name _____ Date _____

Different Spellings for the /er/ Sound

Read each sentence. Fill in the circle next to the word that correctly completes the sentence.

1. The settlers _____ their first winter in the new land.
   - ● survived
   - ○ servived
   - ○ sirvived

2. The students learned to _____ a computer.
   - ○ opirate
   - ○ opurate
   - ● operate

3. The road curved _____ over the mountain.
   - ○ upword
   - ● upward
   - ○ upwird

4. Birds _____ as the sun came up.
   - ● chirped
   - ○ cherped
   - ○ churped

5. One of my favorite subjects is _____.
   - ○ histery
   - ○ histury
   - ● history

6. Lottie holds the school _____ for running a mile.
   - ○ recird
   - ● record
   - ○ recurd

7. This is the most _____ way to get to the swimming pool.
   - ○ durect
   - ○ darect
   - ● direct

8. It was a _____ day for a baseball game.
   - ○ perfict
   - ○ purfect
   - ● perfect

9. Everything in this store costs less than a _____ .
   - ● dollar
   - ○ doller
   - ○ dollir

10. People _____ to their cars as soon as it started raining.
    - ○ herried
    - ● hurried
    - ○ hirried

Diagnostic Assessment

Consonant Before -*le* Spelling Pattern

Read each sentence. Fill in the circle next to the correct spelling of the word that completes the sentence. Remember that -*le*, -*al*, -*il*, -*ol*, and -*el* are all spellings of the same sound.

1. Scientists fight a _____ against disease every day.
   ○ battel   ○ battil   ○ battle

2. The _____ wrote the correct answer on the board.
   ○ puple   ○ pupil   ○ pupol

3. My teacher loved the _____ of my paper.
   ○ tital   ○ titul   ○ title

4. Getting up the hill was a _____ because of the wind.
   ○ struggle   ○ struggel   ○ struggal

5. The _____ is the head of the school.
   ○ principol   ○ principal   ○ principle

6. I peeled the _____ from the soup can.
   ○ label   ○ labol   ○ labil

7. That _____ makes the room look warm.
   ○ candil   ○ candel   ○ candle

8. Idle and _____ are homophones.
   ○ idal   ○ idel   ○ idol

9. Fixing the broken window is no _____ at all.
   ○ trouble   ○ troubil   ○ troubel

10. This is a good _____ of how well Nancy can draw.
    ○ exampul   ○ example   ○ exampil

Diagnostic Assessment   **91**

Consonant Before -*le* Spelling Pattern

Read each sentence. Fill in the circle next to the correct
spelling of the word that completes the sentence. Remember
that -*le*, -*al*, -*il*, -*ol*, and -*el* are all spellings of the same
sound.

1. Scientists fight a _____ against disease every day.
    ○ battel   ○ battil   ● battle

2. The _____ wrote the correct answer on the board.
    ○ puple   ● pupil   ○ pupol

3. My teacher loved the _____ of my paper.
    ○ tital   ○ titul   ● title

4. Getting up the hill was a _____ because of the wind.
    ● struggle   ○ struggel   ○ struggal

5. The _____ is the head of the school.
    ○ principol   ● principal   ○ principle

6. I peeled the _____ from the soup can.
    ● label   ○ labol   ○ labil

7. That _____ makes the room look warm.
    ○ candil   ○ candel   ● candle

8. Idle and _____ are homophones.
    ○ idal   ○ idel   ● idol

9. Fixing the broken window is no _____ at all.
    ● trouble   ○ troubil   ○ troubel

10. This is a good _____ of how well Nancy can draw.
    ○ exampul   ● example   ○ exampil

Diagnostic Assessment

Frequently Misspelled Words

Read each sentence. Fill in the circle next to the word that is spelled correctly to complete the sentence.

1. Drew's favorite _____ has pictures of mountains.
   - ○ calendar
   - ○ calender
   - ○ kalendar

2. Simon is a young _____ who is interested in science.
   - ○ skolar
   - ○ scholar
   - ○ scolar

3. Our zoo just acquired two _____ kinds of wild goats called an ibex and a markhor.
   - ○ unusual
   - ○ unussual
   - ○ unusuall

4. My name is mentioned in the third _____ of this news story.
   - ○ paragraff
   - ○ paragraf
   - ○ paragraph

5. Ted tried to _____ life without his music.
   - ○ imajine
   - ○ imagine
   - ○ imadgine

6. The divers searched for treasure among the _____ of the ship.
   - ○ reckage
   - ○ rreckage
   - ○ wreckage

7. Janna found a small, yellow bird _____ in the bushes.
   - ○ cawght
   - ○ caught
   - ○ cought

8. Grant played _____ golf with his grandfather.
   - ○ miniachure
   - ○ miniasure
   - ○ miniature

9. The _____ complained of a sore toe.
   - ○ patient
   - ○ pachient
   - ○ pashient

10. The tryouts for the musical are from Wednesday _____ Saturday.
    - ○ through
    - ○ throug
    - ○ threw

Frequently Misspelled Words

Read each sentence. Fill in the circle next to the word
that is spelled correctly to complete the sentence.

1. Drew's favorite _____ has pictures of mountains.
   ● calendar   ○ calender   ○ kalendar

2. Simon is a young _____ who is interested in science.
   ○ skolar   ● scholar   ○ scolar

3. Our zoo just acquired two _____ kinds of wild goats
   called an ibex and a markhor.
   ● unusual   ○ unussual   ○ unusuall

4. My name is mentioned in the third _____ of this
   news story.
   ○ paragraff   ○ paragraf   ● paragraph

5. Ted tried to _____ life without his music.
   ○ imajine   ● imagine   ○ imadgine

6. The divers searched for treasure among the _____ of
   the ship.
   ○ reckage   ○ rreckage   ● wreckage

7. Janna found a small, yellow bird _____ in the bushes.
   ○ cawght   ● caught   ○ cought

8. Grant played _____ golf with his grandfather.
   ○ miniachure   ○ miniasure   ● miniature

9. The _____ complained of a sore toe.
   ● patient   ○ pachient   ○ pashient

10. The tryouts for the musical are from Wednesday _____
    Saturday.
    ● through   ○ throug   ○ threw

Consonant Blends and Digraphs

Read each sentence. Fill in the circle next to the word that correctly completes the sentence.

1. My sister likes to _____ before she runs.
   ○ stretch   ○ stech   ○ sctretch

2. The king's _____ was made of gold and rare wood.
   ○ trone   ○ tharone   ○ throne

3. The bus _____ is posted on the wall.
   ○ skedule   ○ schedule   ○ scedule

4. My mother and I _____ the old paint from a door.
   ○ scaped   ○ scraped   ○ schraped

5. The eggs in the nest will _____ soon.
   ○ hatch   ○ hach   ○ hadch

6. While we were flying, I could see the plane's _____ on the ground.
   ○ chadow   ○ shadow   ○ schadow

7. I had to _____ the water out of my towel.
   ○ ring   ○ waring   ○ wring

8. The explorers were mapping the _____ area.
   ○ unown   ○ unnown   ○ unknown

9. Tommy isn't strong _____ to lift that by himself.
   ○ enough   ○ enouf   ○ enought

10. Our basement floods _____ it rains.
    ○ wenever   ○ wehenever   ○ whenever

Consonant Blends and Digraphs

Read each sentence. Fill in the circle next to the word that correctly completes the sentence.

1. My sister likes to _____ before she runs.
   - ● stretch
   - ○ stech
   - ○ sctretch

2. The king's _____ was made of gold and rare wood.
   - ○ trone
   - ○ tharone
   - ● throne

3. The bus _____ is posted on the wall.
   - ○ skedule
   - ● schedule
   - ○ scedule

4. My mother and I _____ the old paint from a door.
   - ○ scaped
   - ● scraped
   - ○ schraped

5. The eggs in the nest will _____ soon.
   - ● hatch
   - ○ hach
   - ○ hadch

6. While we were flying, I could see the plane's _____ on the ground.
   - ○ chadow
   - ● shadow
   - ○ schadow

7. I had to _____ the water out of my towel.
   - ○ ring
   - ○ waring
   - ● wring

8. The explorers were mapping the _____ area.
   - ○ unown
   - ○ unnown
   - ● unknown

9. Tommy isn't strong _____ to lift that by himself.
   - ● enough
   - ○ enouf
   - ○ enought

10. Our basement floods _____ it rains.
    - ○ wenever
    - ○ wehenever
    - ● whenever

Diagnostic Assessment

Homophones

Read each sentence. Fill in the circle next to the pair of words that best completes the sentence.

1. The _____ was _____ to use the family's swimming pool after lunch.
   - ○ maid, allowed
   - ○ made, allowed
   - ○ maid, aloud
   - ○ made, aloud

2. You _____ to have the _____ replaced on those shoes.
   - ○ knead, heels
   - ○ need, heals
   - ○ need, heels
   - ○ knead, heals

3. Grandpa _____ the _____ to stakes for support.
   - ○ tide, rose
   - ○ tied, rows
   - ○ tide, rows
   - ○ tied, rose

4. Shelly has _____ arrangements for a _____ to Alaska.
   - ○ made, crews
   - ○ made, cruise
   - ○ maid, crews
   - ○ maid, cruise

5. All four work _____ must _____ at 10:15 for a break.
   - ○ cruise, pause
   - ○ cruise, paws
   - ○ crews, paws
   - ○ crews, pause

6. "Time _____ all wounds," I said _____, though I meant only to whisper it.
   - ○ heals, allowed
   - ○ heals, aloud
   - ○ heels, allowed
   - ○ heels, aloud

7. With their dirty _____, the cats had left three _____ of muddy prints.
   - ○ paws, rose
   - ○ pause, rose
   - ○ paws, rows
   - ○ pause, rows

Homophones

**Read each sentence. Fill in the circle next to the pair
of words that best completes the sentence.**

1. The _____ was _____ to use the family's swimming
   pool after lunch.
   - ● maid, allowed ○ maid, aloud
   - ○ made, allowed ○ made, aloud

2. You _____ to have the _____ replaced on those
   shoes.
   - ○ knead, heels ● need, heels
   - ○ need, heals ○ knead, heals

3. Grandpa _____ the _____ to stakes for support.
   - ○ tide, rose ○ tide, rows
   - ○ tied, rows ● tied, rose

4. Shelly has _____ arrangements for a _____ to
   Alaska.
   - ○ made, crews ○ maid, crews
   - ● made, cruise ○ maid, cruise

5. All four work _____ must _____ at 10:15 for
   a break.
   - ○ cruise, pause ○ crews, paws
   - ○ cruise, paws ● crews, pause

6. "Time _____ all wounds," I said _____, though I
   meant only to whisper it.
   - ○ heals, allowed ○ heels, allowed
   - ● heals, aloud ○ heels, aloud

7. With their dirty _____, the cats had left three _____
   of muddy prints.
   - ○ paws, rose ● paws, rows
   - ○ pause, rose ○ pause, rows

Diagnostic Assessment

Long-Vowel Spellings

Read each sentence. Fill in the circle next to the long-vowel word that correctly completes the sentence.

1. The _____ train had more than a hundred cars.
   - ○ frait
   - ○ frate
   - ○ freight

2. Some squirrels built a nest in the _____ tree.
   - ○ holloe
   - ○ hollow
   - ○ hollo

3. _____ of the teams played very well.
   - ○ Niether
   - ○ Neether
   - ○ Neither

4. The students will _____ the butterflies they raised.
   - ○ release
   - ○ releese
   - ○ realese

5. The _____ of Maine is often rocky.
   - ○ coost
   - ○ coast
   - ○ coste

6. None of Hal's friends _____ he had caught such a big fish.
   - ○ believed
   - ○ beleeved
   - ○ beleaved

7. Science has helped farmers _____ more food.
   - ○ proaduce
   - ○ prooduce
   - ○ produce

8. My family is _____ about going on vacation.
   - ○ exceited
   - ○ excyted
   - ○ excited

9. Karen tried to _____ how to do the experiment.
   - ○ explain
   - ○ explane
   - ○ explean

10. In the story, the explorers took a _____ to the moon.
    - ○ journie
    - ○ journey
    - ○ journee

Long-Vowel Spellings

Read each sentence. Fill in the circle next to the long-vowel word that correctly completes the sentence.

1. The _____ train had more than a hundred cars.
   - ○ frait
   - ○ frate
   - ● freight

2. Some squirrels built a nest in the _____ tree.
   - ○ holloe
   - ● hollow
   - ○ hollo

3. _____ of the teams played very well.
   - ○ Niether
   - ○ Neether
   - ● Neither

4. The students will _____ the butterflies they raised.
   - ● release
   - ○ releese
   - ○ realese

5. The _____ of Maine is often rocky.
   - ○ coost
   - ● coast
   - ○ coste

6. None of Hal's friends _____ he had caught such a big fish.
   - ● believed
   - ○ beleeved
   - ○ beleaved

7. Science has helped farmers _____ more food.
   - ○ proaduce
   - ○ prooduce
   - ● produce

8. My family is _____ about going on vacation.
   - ○ exceited
   - ○ excyted
   - ● excited

9. Karen tried to _____ how to do the experiment.
   - ● explain
   - ○ explane
   - ○ explean

10. In the story, the explorers took a _____ to the moon.
    - ○ journie
    - ● journey
    - ○ journee

Diagnostic Assessment

Vocabulary

Vocabulary

The assessments in this section are intended to be completed by a student working independently. The pages for these assessments should be duplicated and distributed to the student. You may find it helpful to read the directions for these assessments out loud before they are administered to ensure that the student understands what to do.

Duplicate the "Student Record" form on page 10 and complete the record for each assessment. You can calculate the percentage correct by hand or look it up in the percentage chart on the inside back cover of this guide. The "Student Record" has space for you to record the observations you make while the student is completing the assessment. Note things such as the speed with which the student works, signs of frustration, attempts at self-correction, and other relevant behaviors.

If some students are having difficulty reading, you may choose to administer the assessments orally. One possibility is to read the assessment to the student and have the student fill in the correct answer. Another possibility is to read the assessment with the student. Allow the student to begin reading, and when the student encounters difficulty, read along with the student until he or she begins reading fluently again.

You may enhance either method of assessment—student reading silently or with your assistance—by asking the student questions like "How do you know that?" or "What makes you sure this answer is right?" The student's answers to these follow-up questions can give you further insight into his or her understanding of the task and his or her ability to read with understanding.

The following chart provides an assessment guideline for each of the fifth-grade Vocabulary assessments.

Assessment	Estimated Percentiles		
	0–49	50–79	80+
Word Families (p. 103)	0–7	8–11	12–15
Content-Area Words (p. 105)	0–3	4–5	6
Regular and Irregular Plurals (p. 107)	0–4	5–7	8–9
Words with Multiple Meanings (p. 109)	0–3	4–5	6
Compound Words (p. 111)	0–7	8–11	12–15
Synonyms and Antonyms (p. 113)	0–3	4–5	6–7

Word Families

Read each group of words. Fill in the circle next to the answer that is not in the same word family as the other answers.

1. ○ jury   ○ jurisdiction   ○ juvenile   ○ jurist

2. ○ flavorful   ○ flavor   ○ flavoring   ○ frivolous

3. ○ motherhood   ○ motion   ○ motive   ○ motivate

4. ○ divide   ○ divisor   ○ dividend   ○ divine

5. ○ socket   ○ social   ○ society   ○ socialize

6. ○ appear   ○ appeared   ○ appease   ○ appearance

7. ○ operation   ○ opponent   ○ operate   ○ operator

8. ○ timekeeper   ○ timeless   ○ timid   ○ timetable

9. ○ literature   ○ live   ○ lively   ○ livable

10. ○ harmonica   ○ harmonious   ○ harmless   ○ harmony

11. ○ compete   ○ competition   ○ competitor   ○ command

12. ○ observe   ○ observatory   ○ obvious   ○ observation

13. ○ finish   ○ foolish   ○ foolproof   ○ foolhardy

14. ○ useful   ○ usher   ○ useless   ○ usable

15. ○ fulfill   ○ fulfilling   ○ fulfillment   ○ fullback

Word Families

Read each group of words. Fill in the circle next to the answer that is not in the same word family as the other answers.

1. ○ jury ○ jurisdiction ● juvenile ○ jurist

2. ○ flavorful ○ flavor ○ flavoring ● frivolous

3. ● motherhood ○ motion ○ motive ○ motivate

4. ○ divide ○ divisor ○ dividend ● divine

5. ● socket ○ social ○ society ○ socialize

6. ○ appear ○ appeared ● appease ○ appearance

7. ○ operation ● opponent ○ operate ○ operator

8. ○ timekeeper ○ timeless ● timid ○ timetable

9. ● literature ○ live ○ lively ○ livable

10. ○ harmonica ○ harmonious ● harmless ○ harmony

11. ○ compete ○ competition ○ competitor ● command

12. ○ observe ○ observatory ● obvious ○ observation

13. ● finish ○ foolish ○ foolproof ○ foolhardy

14. ○ useful ● usher ○ useless ○ usable

15. ○ fulfill ○ fulfilling ○ fulfillment ● fullback

Diagnostic Assessment

Content-Area Words

Read each item. Fill in the circle next to the answer you think is best.

1. Storks migrate from Europe to Africa and back each year.
   Migrate is closest in meaning to
   ○ appear.
   ○ rest.
   ○ travel.

2. The Big Dipper is a constellation almost everyone knows.
   A constellation is a
   ○ star that is very bright.
   ○ group of stars.
   ○ star that appears suddenly.

3. During periods of great cold, a glacier covered much of North
   America. A glacier is a
   ○ huge jungle.
   ○ sheet of ice.
   ○ dry desert.

4. The doctor made an incision to begin the operation.
   An incision is a kind of
   ○ cut.
   ○ scar.
   ○ sickness.

5. The dictator was not liked by the people in the country.
   A dictator is
   ○ an unusually autocratic ruler.
   ○ a kind president.
   ○ a just king.

6. The orchestra played the overture at the beginning of the
   opera. An overture is
   ○ a musical instrument.
   ○ a play in which actors wear makeup.
   ○ a kind of musical composition.

Content-Area Words

Read each item. Fill in the circle next to the answer you think is best.

1. Storks migrate from Europe to Africa and back each year.
   Migrate is closest in meaning to
   ○ appear.
   ○ rest.
   ● travel.

2. The Big Dipper is a constellation almost everyone knows.
   A constellation is a
   ○ star that is very bright.
   ● group of stars.
   ○ star that appears suddenly.

3. During periods of great cold, a glacier covered much of North
   America. A glacier is a
   ○ huge jungle.
   ● sheet of ice.
   ○ dry desert.

4. The doctor made an incision to begin the operation.
   An incision is a kind of
   ● cut.
   ○ scar.
   ○ sickness.

5. The dictator was not liked by the people in the country.
   A dictator is
   ● an unusually autocratic ruler.
   ○ a kind president.
   ○ a just king.

6. The orchestra played the overture at the beginning of the
   opera. An overture is
   ○ a musical instrument.
   ○ a play in which actors wear makeup.
   ● a kind of musical composition.

Regular and Irregular Plurals

Read each sentence. Fill in the circle next to the correct plural form of the word to complete the sentence.

1. The _____ of the tests will be available on Thursday.
   - ○ resultes   ○ resultts   ○ results   ○ resultss

2. The _____ of that company have been under investigation.
   - ○ activitys   ○ activities   ○ activityes   ○ activityys

3. All the _____ in the coastal city hit by Hurricane Hannah were destroyed.
   - ○ wharffs   ○ wharfes   ○ wharfen   ○ wharves

4. Roger put too many _____ in this green salad.
   - ○ radishes   ○ radish   ○ radishs   ○ radeesh

5. Twenty-four Canadian _____ flew gracefully over our roof this evening.
   - ○ gooses   ○ goosen   ○ geese   ○ goose

6. The _____ kept close to their mothers while they were out in the field.
   - ○ callfs   ○ calves   ○ calfes   ○ calf

7. This artist's apron has eight _____ for holding supplies.
   - ○ pocketes   ○ pocketts   ○ pocket   ○ pockets

8. Edwin used three different _____ to achieve the high gloss on his classic car.
   - ○ waxes   ○ waxs   ○ waxxes   ○ waxen

9. For the picnic, we will need at least six _____ of sourdough bread.
   - ○ loafs   ○ loaves   ○ loaffs   ○ loafe

Regular and Irregular Plurals

Read each sentence. Fill in the circle next to the correct plural form of the word to complete the sentence.

1. The _____ of the tests will be available on Thursday.
   ○ resultes   ○ resultts   ● results   ○ resultss

2. The _____ of that company have been under investigation.
   ○ activitys   ● activities   ○ activityes   ○ activityys

3. All the _____ in the coastal city hit by Hurricane Hannah were destroyed.
   ○ wharffs   ○ wharfes   ○ wharfen   ● wharves

4. Roger put too many _____ in this green salad.
   ● radishes   ○ radish   ○ radishs   ○ radeesh

5. Twenty-four Canadian _____ flew gracefully over our roof this evening.
   ○ gooses   ○ goosen   ● geese   ○ goose

6. The _____ kept close to their mothers while they were out in the field.
   ○ callfs   ● calves   ○ calfes   ○ calf

7. This artist's apron has eight _____ for holding supplies.
   ○ pocketes   ○ pocketts   ○ pocket   ● pockets

8. Edwin used three different _____ to achieve the high gloss on his classic car.
   ● waxes   ○ waxs   ○ waxxes   ○ waxen

9. For the picnic, we will need at least six _____ of sourdough bread.
   ○ loafs   ● loaves   ○ loaffs   ○ loafe

Words with Multiple Meanings

Read each question. Fill in the circle next to the answer you think is correct.

1. In which sentence does the word <u>throw</u> mean "to toss with your hand"?
   - ○ Don't <u>throw</u> the switch until I'm out of the way.
   - ○ An athlete always should play to win and never <u>throw</u> a game.
   - ○ Jamie can <u>throw</u> a football really far.

2. In which sentence does the word <u>front</u> mean "first"?
   - ○ The <u>front</u> of the building was just painted.
   - ○ The <u>front</u> row in a movie theater is usually empty.
   - ○ The car in <u>front</u> of ours had a flat tire.

3. In which sentence does the word <u>cut</u> mean "to use a knife"?
   - ○ You can <u>cut</u> an hour from your trip if you follow the river.
   - ○ Jasmine made the <u>cut</u> and is on the basketball team.
   - ○ You should <u>cut</u> the apple into four pieces.

4. In which sentence does the word <u>dish</u> mean "something you eat from"?
   - ○ The <u>dish</u> broke when I dropped it.
   - ○ It takes about an hour to make this vegetable <u>dish</u>.
   - ○ We get our television through a satellite <u>dish</u>.

5. In which sentence does the word <u>ring</u> mean "something you wear"?
   - ○ The circus <u>ring</u> was filled with clowns.
   - ○ This <u>ring</u> is too small for Harriet now.
   - ○ It's hard to hear the phone <u>ring</u> in this room.

6. In which sentence does the word <u>drop</u> mean "a very small amount"?
   - ○ Be careful or you'll <u>drop</u> the tray.
   - ○ There wasn't a <u>drop</u> of soup left in my bowl when I was finished.
   - ○ The <u>drop</u> from the top of the cliff to the bottom was more than a hundred feet.

Words with Multiple Meanings

Read each question. Fill in the circle next to the answer you think is correct.

1. In which sentence does the word <u>throw</u> mean "to toss with your hand"?

   ○ Don't <u>throw</u> the switch until I'm out of the way.
   ○ An athlete always should play to win and never <u>throw</u> a game.
   ● Jamie can <u>throw</u> a football really far.

2. In which sentence does the word <u>front</u> mean "first"?

   ○ The <u>front</u> of the building was just painted.
   ● The <u>front</u> row in a movie theater is usually empty.
   ○ The car in <u>front</u> of ours had a flat tire.

3. In which sentence does the word <u>cut</u> mean "to use a knife"?

   ○ You can <u>cut</u> an hour from your trip if you follow the river.
   ○ Jasmine made the <u>cut</u> and is on the basketball team.
   ● You should <u>cut</u> the apple into four pieces.

4. In which sentence does the word <u>dish</u> mean "something you eat from"?

   ● The <u>dish</u> broke when I dropped it.
   ○ It takes about an hour to make this vegetable <u>dish</u>.
   ○ We get our television through a satellite <u>dish</u>.

5. In which sentence does the word <u>ring</u> mean "something you wear"?

   ○ The circus <u>ring</u> was filled with clowns.
   ● This <u>ring</u> is too small for Harriet now.
   ○ It's hard to hear the phone <u>ring</u> in this room.

6. In which sentence does the word <u>drop</u> mean "a very small amount"?

   ○ Be careful or you'll <u>drop</u> the tray.
   ● There wasn't a <u>drop</u> of soup left in my bowl when I was finished.
   ○ The <u>drop</u> from the top of the cliff to the bottom was more than a hundred feet.

Compound Words

Read each group of words. Fill in the circle next
to the compound word in each group.

1. ○ wildcat ○ northern ○ sentence

2. ○ ice cream ○ freedom ○ delicious

3. ○ divide ○ measure ○ lighthouse

4. ○ shake-up ○ dangerous ○ rodeo

5. ○ important ○ gift shop ○ department

6. ○ companies ○ ice skate ○ direction

7. ○ ordinary ○ include ○ cookbook

8. ○ wonderful ○ cross-reference ○ statement

9. ○ suggested ○ tomorrow ○ airport

10. ○ user-friendly ○ frequent ○ program

11. ○ letter ○ package ○ post office

12. ○ up-to-date ○ festive ○ delightful

13. ○ decode ○ light bulb ○ reflect

14. ○ old-fashioned ○ parachute ○ history

15. ○ seasonal ○ lemonade ○ swimming pool

Name _____ Date _____

Compound Words

Read each group of words. Fill in the circle next
to the compound word in each group.

1. ● wildcat   ○ northern   ○ sentence

2. ● ice cream   ○ freedom   ○ delicious

3. ○ divide   ○ measure   ● lighthouse

4. ● shake-up   ○ dangerous   ○ rodeo

5. ○ important   ● gift shop   ○ department

6. ○ companies   ● ice skate   ○ direction

7. ○ ordinary   ○ include   ● cookbook

8. ○ wonderful   ● cross-reference   ○ statement

9. ○ suggested   ○ tomorrow   ● airport

10. ● user-friendly   ○ frequent   ○ program

11. ○ letter   ○ package   ● post office

12. ● up-to-date   ○ festive   ○ delightful

13. ○ decode   ● light bulb   ○ reflect

14. ● old-fashioned   ○ parachute   ○ history

15. ○ seasonal   ○ lemonade   ● swimming pool

Diagnostic Assessment

Synonyms and Antonyms

For Numbers 1 through 4, read each sentence. Fill in the circle next to the word that is a synonym for the underlined word.

1. The army was arranged in ranks, facing the <u>enemy</u>.
   - ○ friend
   - ○ horizon
   - ○ battle
   - ○ foe

2. His <u>disgrace</u> was known by everyone.
   - ○ face
   - ○ reputation
   - ○ shame
   - ○ esteem

3. His journey left him <u>weary</u>.
   - ○ happy
   - ○ tired
   - ○ rested
   - ○ suspicious

4. The new sports stadium is <u>big</u>.
   - ○ miniature
   - ○ enormous
   - ○ round
   - ○ ugly

Read each sentence. Fill in the circle next to the word that is an antonym for the underlined word.

5. <u>Notice</u> the pictures on the page.
   - ○ see
   - ○ color
   - ○ ignore
   - ○ observe

6. The expensive dress was a <u>luxury</u>.
   - ○ necessity
   - ○ joy
   - ○ delight
   - ○ present

7. The instructions are <u>complicated</u>.
   - ○ difficult
   - ○ simple
   - ○ wrong
   - ○ silly

Synonyms and Antonyms

For Numbers 1 through 4, read each sentence. Fill in
the circle next to the word that is a synonym for the
underlined word.

1. The army was arranged in ranks, facing the <u>enemy</u>.
   - ○ friend
   - ○ horizon
   - ○ battle
   - ● foe

2. His <u>disgrace</u> was known by everyone.
   - ○ face
   - ○ reputation
   - ● shame
   - ○ esteem

3. His journey left him <u>weary</u>.
   - ○ happy
   - ● tired
   - ○ rested
   - ○ suspicious

4. The new sports stadium is <u>big</u>.
   - ○ miniature
   - ● enormous
   - ○ round
   - ○ ugly

Read each sentence. Fill in the circle next to the word
that is an antonym for the underlined word.

5. <u>Notice</u> the pictures on the page.
   - ○ see
   - ○ color
   - ● ignore
   - ○ observe

6. The expensive dress was a <u>luxury</u>.
   - ● necessity
   - ○ joy
   - ○ delight
   - ○ present

7. The instructions are <u>complicated</u>.
   - ○ difficult
   - ● simple
   - ○ wrong
   - ○ silly

Diagnostic Assessment

Silent Reading Comprehension

Silent Reading Comprehension

The assessments in this section are intended to be completed by a student working independently. The pages for these assessments should be duplicated and distributed to the student. You may find it helpful to read the directions for these assessments out loud before they are administered to ensure that the student understands what to do.

Duplicate the "Student Record" form on page 10 and complete the record for each assessment. You can calculate the percentage correct by hand or look it up in the percentage chart on the inside back cover of this guide. The "Student Record" has space for you to record the observations you make while the student is completing the assessment. Note things such as the speed with which the student works, signs of frustration, attempts at self-correction, and other relevant behaviors.

If some students are having difficulty reading, you may choose to administer the assessments orally. One possibility is to read the assessment to the student and have the student fill in the correct answer. Another possibility is to read the assessment with the student. Allow the student to begin reading, and when the student encounters difficulty, read along with the student until he or she begins reading fluently again.

You may enhance either method of assessment—student reading silently or with your assistance—by asking the student questions like "How do you know that?" or "What makes you sure this answer is right?" The student's answers to these follow-up questions can give you further insight into his or her understanding of the task and his or her ability to read with understanding.

The following chart provides an assessment guideline for each of the fifth-grade Silent Reading Comprehension assessments.

Assessment	Estimated Percentiles		
	0–49	50–79	80+
Plot (p. 117)	0–1	2–3	4
Making Inferences (p. 119)	0–1	2	3
Main Idea and Details (p. 121)	0–1	2	3
Cause and Effect (p. 123)	0–1	2–3	4
Sequence (p. 125)	0–3	4–5	6
Analyzing Character Traits (p. 127)	0–1	2–3	4

Plot

Read the story summary. Fill in the circle next to the correct answer to each question.

Dinah and her dog Ralph are lost in the woods. More than two hours have passed since she and Ralph left camp to explore the woods. She had promised her parents that she would stay near camp, but there are so many fascinating things to see in the woods that she has gone farther than she had intended.

Dinah tries to retrace her path, but she succeeds only in going deeper into the woods. She considers making a fire as a signal, but there is no clearing where a fire might be lit safely. The sun is setting, and Dinah becomes frightened. Then Ralph begins to bark and tug at her sleeve. Dinah follows Ralph, who leads her back to the camp and her worried parents. That night, Dinah's mother gives Ralph a large bone to chew and her father declares him a "Hero Dog."

1. What problem is introduced at the beginning of the story?
   ○ Dinah is angry with her parents.
   ○ Dinah is lost in the woods.
   ○ Dinah is lost in a cave.

2. Which of these is not a conflict that Dinah faces?
   ○ Dinah goes deeper into the woods.
   ○ Dinah cannot safely build a campfire.
   ○ Ralph falls into a stream.

3. What is the climax of the story?
   ○ Dinah's parents find her.
   ○ Dinah finds a compass.
   ○ Ralph leads Dinah back to camp.

4. What is the conclusion of the story?
   ○ Ralph gets a bone to chew and is named a "Hero Dog."
   ○ Dinah's parents scold her for getting lost.
   ○ Dinah goes to sleep.

Plot

**Read the story summary. Fill in the circle next to the
correct answer to each question.**

Dinah and her dog Ralph are lost in the woods. More than
two hours have passed since she and Ralph left camp to
explore the woods. She had promised her parents that she
would stay near camp, but there are so many fascinating
things to see in the woods that she has gone farther than she
had intended.

Dinah tries to retrace her path, but she succeeds only in
going deeper into the woods. She considers making a fire as a
signal, but there is no clearing where a fire might be lit safely.
The sun is setting, and Dinah becomes frightened. Then Ralph
begins to bark and tug at her sleeve. Dinah follows Ralph,
who leads her back to the camp and her worried parents.
That night, Dinah's mother gives Ralph a large bone to chew
and her father declares him a "Hero Dog."

1. What problem is introduced at the beginning of the story?
   - ○ Dinah is angry with her parents.
   - ● Dinah is lost in the woods.
   - ○ Dinah is lost in a cave.

2. Which of these is not a conflict that Dinah faces?
   - ○ Dinah goes deeper into the woods.
   - ○ Dinah cannot safely build a campfire.
   - ● Ralph falls into a stream.

3. What is the climax of the story?
   - ○ Dinah's parents find her.
   - ○ Dinah finds a compass.
   - ● Ralph leads Dinah back to camp.

4. What is the conclusion of the story?
   - ● Ralph gets a bone to chew and is named a "Hero Dog."
   - ○ Dinah's parents scold her for getting lost.
   - ○ Dinah goes to sleep.

Making Inferences

Read the story and the questions. Fill in the circle next to the best answer to each question.

Tara trudged along with the rest of her family. They were on what her mother called "the grand tour" of what Tara called a "national nightmare." Every park, monument, and forest in the universe was on their itinerary.

Today's torture was a place called Mesa Verde, and Tara didn't know or care if it was in Colorado, New Mexico, Utah, or Arizona. She wished she was surfing, sailing, playing tennis, or playing basketball with her friends in Daytona Beach, Florida. She wished she was doing anything but this.

Tara's parents shepherded her brothers and her onto an overlook where a few people had gathered. A cliff dwelling tour was to begin there. Tara dragged her feet as she walked over to the edge. Then she looked over. What she saw took her breath away. There in the valley below was a small town carved into a huge, overhanging cliff. It was the most remarkable thing she had ever seen.

1. What can you infer from the first sentence of the story?
   ○ Tara was beginning to enjoy the trip.
   ○ Tara liked her friends better than her family.
   ○ Tara didn't want to be on the trip.

2. What does the second paragraph suggest about Tara?
   ○ She doesn't like geography.
   ○ She enjoys playing sports.
   ○ The family vacations in Florida.

3. What happens when Tara looks over the edge into the valley?
   ○ She understands how Native Americans lived.
   ○ The height makes her stomach feel queasy.
   ○ Her attitude about the trip changes.

Making Inferences

Read the story and the questions. Fill in the circle next to the best answer to each question.

Tara trudged along with the rest of her family. They were on what her mother called "the grand tour" of what Tara called a "national nightmare." Every park, monument, and forest in the universe was on their itinerary.

Today's torture was a place called Mesa Verde, and Tara didn't know or care if it was in Colorado, New Mexico, Utah, or Arizona. She wished she was surfing, sailing, playing tennis, or playing basketball with her friends in Daytona Beach, Florida. She wished she was doing anything but this.

Tara's parents shepherded her brothers and her onto an overlook where a few people had gathered. A cliff dwelling tour was to begin there. Tara dragged her feet as she walked over to the edge. Then she looked over. What she saw took her breath away. There in the valley below was a small town carved into a huge, overhanging cliff. It was the most remarkable thing she had ever seen.

1. What can you infer from the first sentence of the story?
   - ○ Tara was beginning to enjoy the trip.
   - ○ Tara liked her friends better than her family.
   - ● Tara didn't want to be on the trip.

2. What does the second paragraph suggest about Tara?
   - ○ She doesn't like geography.
   - ● She enjoys playing sports.
   - ○ The family vacations in Florida.

3. What happens when Tara looks over the edge into the valley?
   - ○ She understands how Native Americans lived.
   - ○ The height makes her stomach feel queasy.
   - ● Her attitude about the trip changes.

Diagnostic Assessment

Main Idea and Details

**Read the story and the questions. Fill in the circle next
to the best answer to each question.**

The Inca nation was one of the most highly organized Native American
nations. The Inca created a vast, well-organized society in the mountains of
South America in the region now known as Peru. They built a vast highway
system that improved transportation and communication. The Inca did not have
a written language, but they created a unique form of communication called
quipu. Runners traversed the highways carrying quipus, which were devices
composed of specially knotted strings that were deciphered to relay messages.

The Incan army earned a reputation for efficiency. Once the Inca
conquered a village, they allowed the village to join the empire peacefully
by allowing the villagers to keep their customs and deities. However, the
Inca expected the conquered villages to add Incan customs and deities to
their own. The Inca also expected conquered villages to pay tribute to
Sappa Inca, the ruler of the empire.

The Sappa Inca was respected as a wise and powerful descendant of
the Sun god. Tribute was paid in gold, grain, and labor, and much of it went
to build and maintain Incan temples. A portion of the grain tribute was
redistributed to the people during emergencies, such as crop failures or
earthquakes, so no one in the Incan empire ever went hungry.

1. What is the main idea of this article?
   ○ It is hard to communicate or transport goods in the mountains.
   ○ The Incan empire was well organized.
   ○ The Incan army was not as violent as the Aztec army.

2. The Incan army's reputation for efficiency contributed to the
   growth and order of the empire by
   ○ continuous fighting.
   ○ the punishments it inflicted upon the people it conquered.
   ○ encouraging villages to join the empire peacefully.

3. What does the final sentence in the article suggest?
   ○ The people were forced to pay high tribute, but they still had
     enough to eat.
   ○ The Incan empire grew less grain than it needed.
   ○ The empire's emergency plan benefited the people.

Diagnostic Assessment **121**

Main Idea and Details

**Read the story and the questions. Fill in the circle next
to the best answer to each question.**

The Inca nation was one of the most highly organized Native American
nations. The Inca created a vast, well-organized society in the mountains of
South America in the region now known as Peru. They built a vast highway
system that improved transportation and communication. The Inca did not have
a written language, but they created a unique form of communication called
quipu. Runners traversed the highways carrying quipus, which were devices
composed of specially knotted strings that were deciphered to relay messages.

The Incan army earned a reputation for efficiency. Once the Inca
conquered a village, they allowed the village to join the empire peacefully
by allowing the villagers to keep their customs and deities. However, the
Inca expected the conquered villages to add Incan customs and deities to
their own. The Inca also expected conquered villages to pay tribute to
Sappa Inca, the ruler of the empire.

The Sappa Inca was respected as a wise and powerful descendant of
the Sun god. Tribute was paid in gold, grain, and labor, and much of it went
to build and maintain Incan temples. A portion of the grain tribute was
redistributed to the people during emergencies, such as crop failures or
earthquakes, so no one in the Incan empire ever went hungry.

1. What is the main idea of this article?
   - ○ It is hard to communicate or transport goods in the mountains.
   - ● The Incan empire was well organized.
   - ○ The Incan army was not as violent as the Aztec army.

2. The Inca army's reputation for efficiency contributed to the
   growth and order of the empire by
   - ○ continuous fighting.
   - ○ the punishments it inflicted upon the people it conquered.
   - ● encouraging villages to join the empire peacefully.

3. What does the final sentence in the article suggest?
   - ○ The people were forced to pay high tribute, but they still had
     enough to eat.
   - ○ The Incan empire grew less grain than it needed.
   - ● The empire's emergency plan benefited the people.

Cause and Effect

Read the diary entry, then fill in the circle next to the correct answer to each question.

October 17—The day was a complete waste. I did not properly store my equipment in the sailboat. The boat tipped to the side, and then it overturned. All of my equipment fell in the water. I had packed the camera and film in a metal case. The case floated, so I was able to save it. I had not taken the time to pack the video camera in a case, so it sank to the bottom of the bay. I dived to recover it and hit my head on a rock that was hidden by the muddy water. I spent the rest of the day seeing a doctor, finding a new video camera, and cleaning the boat. Tomorrow, I will store the equipment properly in the boat.

1. What event caused the day to be a waste?
   - ○ The sailboat was not properly loaded and it overturned.
   - ○ The video camera sank to the bottom of the bay.
   - ○ The sailboat had a leak.

2. What is one effect of the event?
   - ○ The photograph did not turn out well.
   - ○ The sailboat had to be repaired.
   - ○ The video camera was lost.

3. What is another effect of the event?
   - ○ The sailboat was lost.
   - ○ The film was ruined.
   - ○ The sailboat had to be cleaned.

4. What caused the camera and film to be saved?
   - ○ They were packed in a metal case that floated.
   - ○ They floated.
   - ○ They were not in the sailboat.

Cause and Effect

Read the diary entry, then fill in the circle next to the correct answer to each question.

October 17—The day was a complete waste. I did not properly store my equipment in the sailboat. The boat tipped to the side, and then it overturned. All of my equipment fell in the water. I had packed the camera and film in a metal case. The case floated, so I was able to save it. I had not taken the time to pack the video camera in a case, so it sank to the bottom of the bay. I dived to recover it and hit my head on a rock that was hidden by the muddy water. I spent the rest of the day seeing a doctor, finding a new video camera, and cleaning the boat. Tomorrow, I will store the equipment properly in the boat.

1. What event caused the day to be a waste?
   - ● The sailboat was not properly loaded and it overturned.
   - ○ The video camera sank to the bottom of the bay.
   - ○ The sailboat had a leak.

2. What is one effect of the event?
   - ○ The photograph did not turn out well.
   - ○ The sailboat had to be repaired.
   - ● The video camera was lost.

3. What is another effect of the event?
   - ○ The sailboat was lost.
   - ○ The film was ruined.
   - ● The sailboat had to be cleaned.

4. What caused the camera and film to be saved?
   - ● They were packed in a metal case that floated.
   - ○ They floated.
   - ○ They were not in the sailboat.

Diagnostic Assessment

Name _____ Date _____

Sequence

For Numbers 1 through 3, read each question. Fill in
the circle next to the correct answer.

1. What do indicators of time tell?
- ○ why events occurred when they did
- ○ when events occur
- ○ which event is the most important
- ○ which event is the least important

2. Which of the following words is not an indicator of time?
- ○ yesterday   ○ today   ○ last year   ○ finally

3. Which of the following words is not an indicator of order?
- ○ now   ○ later   ○ whenever   ○ before

The pictures for Numbers 4 through 6 may not be in the
correct order. Choose the indicator of order that goes with
each picture. Fill in the circle next to the correct answer.

4. ○ next summer
   ○ then
   ○ finally
   ○ first

5. ○ first
   ○ next
   ○ tomorrow
   ○ after that

6. ○ at last
   ○ yesterday
   ○ today
   ○ then

Diagnostic Assessment

Sequence

For Numbers 1 through 3, read each question. Fill in
the circle next to the correct answer.

1. What do indicators of time tell?
   - ○ why events occurred when they did
   - ● when events occur
   - ○ which event is the most important
   - ○ which event is the least important

2. Which of the following words is not an indicator of time?
   - ○ yesterday   ○ today   ○ last year   ● finally

3. Which of the following words is not an indicator of order?
   - ○ now   ○ later   ● whenever   ○ before

The pictures for Numbers 4 through 6 may not be in the
correct order. Choose the indicator of order that goes with
each picture. Fill in the circle next to the correct answer.

4. ○ next summer
   ○ then
   ● finally
   ○ first

5. ● first
   ○ next
   ○ tomorrow
   ○ after that

6. ○ at last
   ○ yesterday
   ○ today
   ● then

Analyzing Character Traits

**Read each passage. Fill in the circle next to the word
or phrase that correctly completes the sentence.**

Ian thought about how much he learned from Mrs. Vincent,
who was very demanding. She never let him get away with some
silly story about the dog eating his homework. But Ian couldn't
think of any other teacher who had shown more interest in him.

1. Mrs. Vincent is _____.

○ a good teacher ○ a lazy teacher ○ a selfish teacher

Judy wanted the skirt in the shop window. The skirt cost more
money than she could save from her allowance in a month. So
Judy decided to sew one just like it. Judy's mother gave her some
pretty material from an old dress. Judy drew a skirt pattern on
some butcher paper. In a few hours she had made a skirt that
looked just as nice as the one in the window.

2. Judy is _____.

○ wasteful ○ thrifty ○ cautious

Lillian simply could not seem to finish any job. All she cared
about was her dancing. If her father told her to sweep the porch,
he found her dancing with the broom instead. When she was
supposed to be drying the dishes, she would dance around, waving
the dish cloth in the air, pretending it was a scarf.

3. Lillian is _____.

○ a clown ○ a daydreamer ○ a hard worker

The archaeologist watched Roy, the young volunteer, with
admiration. Roy spent long days in the hot sun digging and sifting.
No one, the archaeologist thought, was more careful in cleaning
the artifacts and in labeling them correctly.

4. Roy is _____.

○ hard working and diligent ○ funny ○ thoughtless

Analyzing Character Traits

**Read each passage. Fill in the circle next to the word
or phrase that correctly completes the sentence.**

Ian thought about how much he learned from Mrs. Vincent,
who was very demanding. She never let him get away with some
silly story about the dog eating his homework. But Ian couldn't
think of any other teacher who had shown more interest in him.

1. Mrs. Vincent is _____.

   ● a good teacher   ○ a lazy teacher   ○ a selfish teacher

Judy wanted the skirt in the shop window. The skirt cost more
money than she could save from her allowance in a month. So
Judy decided to sew one just like it. Judy's mother gave her some
pretty material from an old dress. Judy drew a skirt pattern on
some butcher paper. In a few hours she had made a skirt that
looked just as nice as the one in the window.

2. Judy is _____.

   ○ wasteful   ● thrifty   ○ cautious

Lillian simply could not seem to finish any job. All she cared
about was her dancing. If her father told her to sweep the porch,
he found her dancing with the broom instead. When she was
supposed to be drying the dishes, she would dance around, waving
the dish cloth in the air, pretending it was a scarf.

3. Lillian is _____.

   ○ a clown   ● a daydreamer   ○ a hard worker

The archaeologist watched Roy, the young volunteer, with
admiration. Roy spent long days in the hot sun digging and sifting.
No one, the archaeologist thought, was more careful in cleaning
the artifacts and in labeling them correctly.

4. Roy is _____.

   ● hard working and diligent   ○ funny   ○ thoughtless

Oral Word Reading
Oral Fluency Assessment

Oral Word Reading

Specific instructions for administration are included with each Oral Word Reading assessment. Duplicate the "Student Record" page and give it to the student. Duplicate the scoring page for your use to record each student's scores and any observations.

For instructions on scoring and interpreting these assessments, see Oral Word Reading Introduction.

Oral Fluency Assessment

These directions will help you administer the Oral Fluency Assessments for sixth-grade students. Reproduce the "Student Prompt" page once and save it for use with multiple students. Reproduce the "Student Record" page for each student receiving the assessment. Fill in the name and date information. Give the "Student Prompt" to the student with the following directions:

Say: Here is a story I would like you to read out loud for me. I am going to listen to you read and take some notes. The notes I take will help me learn how well you can read. You will not be graded for this, so you should not feel nervous. Read the story carefully and do your best. Take a few minutes now to look over the story, and then I will tell you when to begin.

Allow time for the student to preview the story. Be sure you have a pen or pencil, the "Student Record," a stopwatch or other timer, and any other materials you may need.

Say: Are you ready? You may begin now.

Start the timer or watch as the student begins to read. You may pronounce any proper nouns with which the student is unfamiliar. Do not count these words as errors

As the student reads, draw a line through each word the student misreads. If possible, note each type of error the student makes by writing it on the "Student Record."

For specific instructions on scoring and interpreting these assessments, see Oral Fluency Introduction.

Oral Word Reading: Student Record
Sixth Grade (Beginning of year)

Name _____   Date _____

make	our	while	look	being
weight	include	group	show	learn
cold	south	difficult	figure	sentence
except	follow	single	developed	possible

Directions

Duplicate page 132 and give it to the student. Duplicate this page and use it as a Student Record for scoring and noting your observations.

Say: Here are some words I would like you to read for me. Read each row of words. If you are not sure how to read a word, take your best guess. You may begin now.

As the student reads, circle each word the student reads wrong. If possible, note the type of error, for example, reading *made* as *mad*. Also, observe the student as she or he reads and record any relevant observations in the space below.

Sixth Grade (Beginning of year)

20 Words   **Number Correct** _____   **Percent Correct** _____

(Multiply the number of correct words by 5 to find the percent correct.)

Observations

_____

_____

_____

_____

_____

Diagnostic Assessment

Oral Word Reading: Student Prompt

make	our	while	look	being
weight	include	group	show	learn
cold	south	difficult	figure	sentence
except	follow	single	developed	possible

 Diagnostic Assessment

Oral Word Reading: Student Record
Sixth Grade (Middle of year)

Name _____ Date _____

shown	heavy	writing	changed	moving
low	general	warm	middle	building
child	study	grow	nothing	simple
floor	straight	covered	attention	trouble

Directions

Duplicate page 134 and give it to the student. Duplicate this page and use it as a Student Record for scoring and noting your observations.

Say: Here are some words I would like you to read for me. Read each row of words. If you are not sure how to read a word, take your best guess. You may begin now.

As the student reads, circle each word the student reads wrong. If possible, note the type of error, for example, reading *made* as *mad*. Also, observe the student as she or he reads and record any relevant observations in the space below.

Sixth Grade (Middle of year)

20 Words   **Number Correct** _____   **Percent Correct** _____

(Multiply the number of correct words by 5 to find the percent correct.)

Observations

_____

_____

_____

_____

_____

_____

Oral Word Reading: Student Prompt

shown	heavy	writing	changed	moving
low	general	warm	middle	building
child	study	grow	nothing	simple
floor	straight	covered	attention	trouble

Diagnostic Assessment

Oral Word Reading: Student Record
Sixth Grade (End of year)

Name _____ Date _____

moment	cause	paper	anyone	chapter
provide	village	purpose	simply	distance
weather	although	strange	meaning	actually
surface	necessary	exactly	business	machine

Directions

Duplicate page 136 and give it to the student. Duplicate this page and use it as a Student Record for scoring and noting your observations.

Say: Here are some words I would like you to read for me. Read each row of words. If you are not sure how to read a word, take your best guess. You may begin now.

As the student reads, circle each word the student reads wrong. If possible, note the type of error, for example, reading *made* as *mad*. Also, observe the student as she or he reads and record any relevant observations in the space below.

Sixth Grade (End of year)

20 Words **Number Correct** _____ **Percent Correct** _____

(Multiply the number of correct words by 5 to find the percent correct.)

Observations

_____

_____

_____

_____

_____

Oral Word Reading: Student Prompt

moment	cause	paper	anyone	chapter
provide	village	purpose	simply	distance
weather	although	strange	meaning	actually
surface	necessary	exactly	business	machine

Diagnostic Assessment

Oral Fluency Assessment: Student Record
Sixth Grade (Beginning of year)

Name _____ **Date** _____

Olympic Dreams

The alarm went off at 5:30 A.M. Chris shut it off and pulled the pillow
over her head. She counted to ten, then slowly got out of bed. She
changed from her pajamas into her bathing suit and warm-up jacket.
With eyes half-open, she walked into the bathroom and brushed her teeth.

A few minutes later, Chris was downstairs, fumbling for her running shoes
under the couch. After putting her shoes on, she grabbed her backpack and
walked into the kitchen. She drank a glass of milk, reached for a banana, and
headed out the door. It was a cool morning, so Chris pulled the hood of her
jacket over her head. She began the one-mile jog to the swimming pool.

When she reached the pool, Chris was already warmed up. She said
hello to the other swimmers, put her stuff in her locker, and walked
to the edge of the pool. Chris put her goggles and hat on, took a
deep breath, and dove into the water. Even though the pool was heated,
it still felt icy because of her run from home to the gym. After
just a few strokes, however, she began warming up.

"Fifty laps times fifty meters is 2500 meters closer to the Olympics,"
Chris thought to herself. It was the same thought she had five mornings
every week. Her friends thought she was crazy, but Chris knew that the
only way to achieve her dream of an Olympic gold medal was this
kind of hard work.

1–14
15–28
29–39
40–51
52–63
64–76
77–91
92–107
108–120
121–132
133–145
146–160
161–173
174–187
188–196
197–208
209–221
222–234
235–247
248–251

EVALUATING CODES FOR ORAL FLUENCY

sky   (/) words read incorrectly

blue
^   sky   (^) inserted word
      ( ]) after the last word

READING RATE AND ACCURACY

Total Words Read: _____

Number of Errors: – _____

Number of Correct Words
Read Per Minute (WPM): _____

Accuracy Rate: _____

READING FLUENCY

	Low	Average	High
Decoding ability	○	○	○
Pace	○	○	○
Syntax	○	○	○
Self-correction	○	○	○
Intonation	○	○	○

Olympic Dreams

The alarm went off at 5:30 A.M. Chris shut it off and pulled the pillow over her head. She counted to ten, then slowly got out of bed. She changed from her pajamas into her bathing suit and warm-up jacket. With eyes half-open, she walked into the bathroom and brushed her teeth.

A few minutes later, Chris was downstairs, fumbling for her running shoes under the couch. After putting her shoes on, she grabbed her backpack and walked into the kitchen. She drank a glass of milk, reached for a banana, and headed out the door. It was a cool morning, so Chris pulled the hood of her jacket over her head. She began the one-mile jog to the swimming pool.

When she reached the pool, Chris was already warmed up. She said hello to the other swimmers, put her stuff in her locker, and walked to the edge of the pool. Chris put her goggles and hat on, took a deep breath, and dove into the water. Even though the pool was heated, it still felt icy because of her run from home to the gym. After just a few strokes, however, she began warming up.

"Fifty laps times fifty meters is 2500 meters closer to the Olympics," Chris thought to herself. It was the same thought she had five mornings every week. Her friends thought she was crazy, but Chris knew that the only way to achieve her dream of an Olympic gold medal was this kind of hard work.

Diagnostic Assessment

Oral Fluency Assessment: Student Record
Sixth Grade (Middle of year)

Name _____ Date _____

Everybody Loves Music

Almost everyone enjoys music of one kind or another. Some people like to   1–13
play music, others like to sing, but many people just like to listen. Maybe   14–27
that is the best thing about music; there are so many ways to enjoy it.   28–42

People seem to have a natural love of music. Babies enjoy soft, slow   43–55
music almost from the time they are born. Every culture on Earth has   56–68
music of one kind or another. In addition, music seems to be as old as   69–83
people themselves. Ever since the beginning of history, people have   84–93
been making music.   94–96

There are many ways of making music, from simply humming or singing   97–108
to playing an instrument. Musical instruments can be something as simple   109–119
as two sticks to a complicated device like an organ, which can have pipes   120–133
more than thirty feet tall. Some musical instruments are so beautiful   134–144
that they seem like works of art.   145–151

Music has a way of bringing people closer. People who like the same kind   152–165
of music will often play together or go to concerts together. In schools all   166–179
over the world, there are groups of young people who play together in bands,   180–193
hoping to become superstars. Groups of adults sing and play in community   194–205
bands, or just get together to sing around a piano. It does not matter how well   206–221
these people sing or play. Music gives all people a chance to come together and   222–236
have a good time.   237–240

**EVALUATING CODES
FOR ORAL FLUENCY**

sky   (/) words read incorrectly

blue
 ^   sky   (^) inserted word
          ( ]) after the last word

READING RATE AND ACCURACY

Total Words Read: _____

Number of Errors: − _____

Number of Correct Words
Read Per Minute (WPM):   _____

Accuracy Rate: _____

READING FLUENCY

	Low	Average	High
Decoding ability	○	○	○
Pace	○	○	○
Syntax	○	○	○
Self-correction	○	○	○
Intonation	○	○	○

Oral Fluency Assessment: Student Prompt

Everybody Loves Music

Almost everyone enjoys music of one kind or another. Some people like to play music, others like to sing, but many people just like to listen. Maybe that is the best thing about music; there are so many ways to enjoy it.

People seem to have a natural love of music. Babies enjoy soft, slow music almost from the time they are born. Every culture on Earth has music of one kind or another. In addition, music seems to be as old as people themselves. Ever since the beginning of history, people have been making music.

There are many ways of making music, from simply humming or singing to playing an instrument. Musical instruments can be something as simple as two sticks to a complicated device like an organ, which can have pipes more than thirty feet tall. Some musical instruments are so beautiful that they seem like works of art.

Music has a way of bringing people closer. People who like the same kind of music will often play together or go to concerts together. In schools all over the world, there are groups of young people who play together in bands, hoping to become superstars. Groups of adults sing and play in community bands, or just get together to sing around a piano. It does not matter how well these people sing or play. Music gives all people a chance to come together and have a good time.

Oral Fluency Assessment: Student Record
Sixth Grade (End of year)

Name _____ **Date** _____

The Cottage

"Dad, can you explain again why we are doing this?" Martin looked at
the vine-covered cottage and let out a sigh. This was the hardest work
he had ever done in his life.

The cottage was at the edge of the large field beside his house. His
family owned the field and lived in a new house by the road. A few
weeks ago, Martin's mother got a letter from an old friend. Since that time,
Martin, his parents, and his brothers and sisters had been clearing weeds
from around the cottage.

"Remember that letter your mother got from Mrs. Howard?" answered
Martin's father. "It said that this cottage was where the Bunnells lived
more than 150 years ago. Zeb and Ann Bunnell began farming here
before the town was built. Some people say that the only reason the town
got started at all was because of them."

"But why are we trying to fix it up?" asked Martin. "Shouldn't the town
be doing this?"

Mr. Jackson thought for a moment before answering. "The town council
might help us out some day, but I don't want to wait for them. There are
some things that we should do on our own, and I think this is one of them.
It just seems like the right thing to do."

Martin sighed again and leaned on his rake. "Dad, I guess we'll be
pleased when the job is done, but right now I'm tired. Can we stop and
have lunch? I think that's the right thing to do."

Line ranges
1–13
14–26
27–33
34–47
48–62
63–76
77–88
89–92
93–102
103–114
115–126
127–140
141–148
149–162
163–165
166–176
177–192
193–209
210–218
219–231
232–246
247–256

EVALUATING CODES FOR ORAL FLUENCY

sky   (/) words read incorrectly

blue

^   sky   (^) inserted word

      ( ]) after the last word

READING RATE AND ACCURACY

Total Words Read: _____

Number of Errors: − _____

Number of Correct Words
Read Per Minute (WPM):   _____

Accuracy Rate: _____

READING FLUENCY

	Low	Average	High
Decoding ability	○	○	○
Pace	○	○	○
Syntax	○	○	○
Self-correction	○	○	○
Intonation	○	○	○

The Cottage

"Dad, can you explain again why we are doing this?" Martin looked at the vine-covered cottage and let out a sigh. This was the hardest work he had ever done in his life.

The cottage was at the edge of the large field beside his house. His family owned the field and lived in a new house by the road. A few weeks ago, Martin's mother got a letter from an old friend. Since that time, Martin, his parents, and his brothers and sisters had been clearing weeds from around the cottage.

"Remember that letter your mother got from Mrs. Howard?" answered Martin's father. "It said that this cottage was where the Bunnells lived more than 150 years ago. Zeb and Ann Bunnell began farming here before the town was built. Some people say that the only reason the town got started at all was because of them."

"But why are we trying to fix it up?" asked Martin. "Shouldn't the town be doing this?"

Mr. Jackson thought for a moment before answering. "The town council might help us out some day, but I don't want to wait for them. There are some things that we should do on our own, and I think this is one of them. It just seems like the right thing to do."

Martin sighed again and leaned on his rake. "Dad, I guess we'll be pleased when the job is done, but right now I'm tired. Can we stop and have lunch? I think that's the right thing to do."

Spelling

The assessments in this section are intended to be completed by a student working independently. The pages for these assessments should be duplicated and distributed to the student. You may find it helpful to read the directions for these assessments out loud before they are administered to ensure that the student understands what to do.

Duplicate the "Student Record" form on page 10 and complete the record for each assessment. You can calculate the percentage correct by hand or look it up in the percentage chart on the inside back cover of this guide. The "Student Record" has space for you to record the observations you make while the student is completing the assessment. Note things such as the speed with which the student works, signs of frustration, attempts at self-correction, and other relevant behaviors.

If some students are having difficulty reading, you may choose to administer the assessments orally. One possibility is to read the assessment to the student and have the student fill in the correct answer. Another possibility is to read the assessment with the student. Allow the student to begin reading, and when the student encounters difficulty, read along with the student until he or she begins reading fluently again.

You may enhance either method of assessment—student reading silently or with your assistance—by asking the student questions like "How do you know that?" or "What makes you sure this answer is right?" The student's answers to these follow-up questions can give you further insight into his or her understanding of the task and his or her ability to read with understanding.

The following chart provides an assessment guideline for each of the sixth-grade Spelling assessments.

Assessment	Estimated Percentiles		
	0–49	50–79	80+
Long-Vowel Spellings (p. 145)	0–5	6–8	9–10
The /er/ Sound (p. 147)	0–5	6–8	9–10
Short-Vowel Spellings (p. 149)	0–5	6–8	9–10
Homophones (p. 151)	0–4	5–6	7–8
Syllables (p. 153)	0–5	6–8	9–10

Long-Vowel Spellings

Read each sentence. Fill in the circle next to the long-vowel word that correctly completes the sentence.

1. The small _____ held on to his mother's skirt.
   ○ cheild   ○ child   ○ childe

2. The bus driver was _____ to give me directions.
   ○ able   ○ aible   ○ aeble

3. Do _____ of you know where the cat is?
   ○ either   ○ iether   ○ ether

4. Water began to _____ from the spring.
   ○ floe   ○ floa   ○ flow

5. We can meet as _____ at nine o'clock.
   ○ ewsual   ○ usual   ○ uesual

6. Grandmother prepared a _____ for Thanksgiving.
   ○ feast   ○ feest   ○ feste

7. It's not a good idea to _____ about what you've done.
   ○ boste   ○ boost   ○ boast

8. Sheri's _____ is in November.
   ○ birthdae   ○ birthday   ○ birthdai

9. Can you please pass me a _____?
   ○ tissu   ○ tissew   ○ tissue

10. The museum was able to _____ that painting.
    ○ acqueir   ○ acquir   ○ acquire

Long-Vowel Spellings

Read each sentence. Fill in the circle next to the long-vowel word that correctly completes the sentence.

1. The small _____ held on to his mother's skirt.
   ○ cheild   ● child   ○ childe

2. The bus driver was _____ to give me directions.
   ● able   ○ aible   ○ aeble

3. Do _____ of you know where the cat is?
   ● either   ○ iether   ○ ether

4. Water began to _____ from the spring.
   ○ floe   ○ floa   ● flow

5. We can meet as _____ at nine o'clock.
   ○ ewsual   ● usual   ○ uesual

6. Grandmother prepared a _____ for Thanksgiving.
   ● feast   ○ feest   ○ feste

7. It's not a good idea to _____ about what you've done.
   ○ boste   ○ boost   ● boast

8. Sheri's _____ is in November.
   ○ birthdae   ● birthday   ○ birthdai

9. Can you please pass me a _____?
   ○ tissu   ○ tissew   ● tissue

10. The museum was able to _____ that painting.
    ○ acqueir   ○ acquir   ● acquire

Diagnostic Assessment

The /er/ Sound

Read each sentence. Fill in the circle next to the word that correctly completes the sentence.

1. Frank read _____ pages of his book yesterday.
   - ○ thirty   ○ therty   ○ thurty

2. It's important to _____ often.
   - ○ exarcise   ○ exurcise   ○ exercise

3. The _____ is always hard to predict.
   - ○ futere   ○ futore   ○ future

4. The library is in that _____.
   - ○ darection   ○ direction   ○ durection

5. Soccer is _____ in our town.
   - ○ popular   ○ populor   ○ populer

6. We can use that yardstick to _____ how tall the plant is.
   - ○ measere   ○ measure   ○ measore

7. The _____ was crowded with ships.
   - ○ harbor   ○ harber   ○ harbir

8. It took a lot of _____ to clean up the basement.
   - ○ effirt   ○ effort   ○ effert

9. Flora's _____ is on the basketball team.
   - ○ brothor   ○ brothir   ○ brother

10. Our science club had a _____ meeting today.
    - ○ regulor   ○ regular   ○ regulir

The /er/ Sound

Read each sentence. Fill in the circle next to the word that correctly completes the sentence.

1. Frank read _____ pages of his book yesterday.
   - ● thirty
   - ○ therty
   - ○ thurty

2. It's important to _____ often.
   - ○ exarcise
   - ○ exurcise
   - ● exercise

3. The _____ is always hard to predict.
   - ○ futere
   - ○ futore
   - ● future

4. The library is in that _____.
   - ○ darection
   - ● direction
   - ○ durection

5. Soccer is _____ in our town.
   - ● popular
   - ○ populor
   - ○ populer

6. We can use that yardstick to _____ how tall the plant is.
   - ○ measere
   - ● measure
   - ○ measore

7. The _____ was crowded with ships.
   - ● harbor
   - ○ harber
   - ○ harbir

8. It took a lot of _____ to clean up the basement.
   - ○ effirt
   - ● effort
   - ○ effert

9. Flora's _____ is on the basketball team.
   - ○ brothor
   - ○ brothir
   - ● brother

10. Our science club had a _____ meeting today.
    - ○ regulor
    - ● regular
    - ○ regulir

Short-Vowel Spellings

Read each sentence. Fill in the circle next to the short-vowel word that correctly completes the sentence.

1. The foresters harvested a small amount of _____ each year.
   - ○ tiember
   - ○ timbere
   - ○ timber

2. Each _____ we sell comes with a guarantee.
   - ○ product
   - ○ producte
   - ○ prowduct

3. Mrs. Parker will _____ the new bank.
   - ○ manige
   - ○ manege
   - ○ manage

4. That house is built on _____ rock.
   - ○ soled
   - ○ solid
   - ○ solide

5. In which _____ of the city do you live?
   - ○ destrict
   - ○ districte
   - ○ district

6. The jury considered the _____.
   - ○ evidence
   - ○ eavidence
   - ○ evedence

7. Now we will _____ the book you just read.
   - ○ descuss
   - ○ discuss
   - ○ discoss

8. A rabbit was _____ in the tall grass.
   - ○ hiedden
   - ○ hiddene
   - ○ hidden

9. Remember to bring your _____ to the football game.
   - ○ jaicket
   - ○ jacket
   - ○ jackit

10. The movie created a realistic sense of _____.
    - ○ terror
    - ○ tearror
    - ○ terrir

Diagnostic Assessment **149**

Short-Vowel Spellings

Read each sentence. Fill in the circle next to the short-vowel word that correctly completes the sentence.

1. The foresters harvested a small amount of _____ each year.
   ○ tiember   ○ timbere   ● timber

2. Each _____ we sell comes with a guarantee.
   ● product   ○ producte   ○ prowduct

3. Mrs. Parker will _____ the new bank.
   ○ manige   ○ manege   ● manage

4. That house is built on _____ rock.
   ○ soled   ● solid   ○ solide

5. In which _____ of the city do you live?
   ○ destrict   ○ districte   ● district

6. The jury considered the _____.
   ● evidence   ○ eavidence   ○ evedence

7. Now we will _____ the book you just read.
   ○ descuss   ● discuss   ○ discoss

8. A rabbit was _____ in the tall grass.
   ○ hiedden   ○ hiddene   ● hidden

9. Remember to bring your _____ to the football game.
   ○ jaicket   ● jacket   ○ jackit

10. The movie created a realistic sense of _____.
    ● terror   ○ tearror   ○ terrir

Homophones

Read each sentence. Fill in the circle next to the pair of words that best completes the sentence.

1. Last summer, we spent a lot of _____ at the _____.
   - ○ time, beach ○ time, beech
   - ○ thyme, beach ○ thyme, beech

2. Glenda was sure about _____ answers, but she _____ at the other two.
   - ○ ate, guest ○ eight, guessed
   - ○ ate, guessed ○ eight, guest

3. After yelling for _____ at the game, Jack was _____.
   - ○ ours, horse ○ ours, hoarse
   - ○ hours, horse ○ hours, hoarse

4. For her birthday, Mona received some _____ earrings and a _____ of jade.
   - ○ pearl, peace ○ purl, piece
   - ○ pearl, piece ○ purl, peace

5. "That stallion is _____!" said the woman, pointing at the beautiful black _____ .
   - ○ hours, hoarse ○ ours, hoarse
   - ○ hours, horse ○ ours, horse

6. In our garden, we have a tall _____ tree and a weather _____ .
   - ○ pare, vein ○ pair, vane
   - ○ pear, vane ○ pear, vein

7. Sharon likes to _____ . She says it gives her a feeling of _____ .
   - ○ right, peace ○ write, peace
   - ○ write, piece ○ right, piece

8. The _____ arrived early and _____ everything in sight.
   - ○ guest, ate ○ guest, eight
   - ○ guessed, ate ○ guessed, eight

Homophones

Read each sentence. Fill in the circle next to the pair of words that best completes the sentence.

1. Last summer, we spent a lot of _____ at the _____.
   - ● time, beach
   - ○ thyme, beach
   - ○ time, beech
   - ○ thyme, beech

2. Glenda was sure about _____ answers, but she _____ at the other two.
   - ○ ate, guest
   - ○ ate, guessed
   - ● eight, guessed
   - ○ eight, guest

3. After yelling for _____ at the game, Jack was _____.
   - ○ ours, horse
   - ○ hours, horse
   - ○ ours, hoarse
   - ● hours, hoarse

4. For her birthday, Mona received some _____ earrings and a _____ of jade.
   - ○ pearl, peace
   - ● pearl, piece
   - ○ purl, piece
   - ○ purl, peace

5. "That stallion is _____!" said the woman, pointing at the beautiful black _____ .
   - ○ hours, hoarse
   - ○ hours, horse
   - ○ ours, hoarse
   - ● ours, horse

6. In our garden, we have a tall _____ tree and a weather _____ .
   - ○ pare, vein
   - ● pear, vane
   - ○ pair, vane
   - ○ pear, vein

7. Sharon likes to _____ . She says it gives her a feeling of _____ .
   - ○ right, peace
   - ○ write, piece
   - ● write, peace
   - ○ right, piece

8. The _____ arrived early and _____ everything in sight.
   - ● guest, ate
   - ○ guessed, ate
   - ○ guest, eight
   - ○ guessed, eight

Diagnostic Assessment

Syllables

For Numbers 1 through 5, read each group of words. Fill in the circle next to the word that is divided correctly into syllables.

1. ○ inter/est   ○ for/mu/la   ○ la/un/dr/y

2. ○ pres/i/dent   ○ stre/ak   ○ penny

3. ○ sque/eze   ○ de/ve/lo/p   ○ a/vail/a/ble

4. ○ reply   ○ ins/ide   ○ de/ny

5. ○ ju/dge   ○ har/mon/i/ca   ○ suburb/an

For Numbers 6 through 10, read each question. Fill in the circle next to the best answer to each question.

6. Which word has three syllables?
   ○ manager   ○ quiet   ○ flipper

7. Which word has the same number of syllables as <u>kangaroo</u>?
   ○ scrape   ○ motion   ○ gentleman

8. Which word has two syllables?
   ○ athletic   ○ dollar   ○ submarine

9. Which word has the same number of syllables as <u>distant</u>?
   ○ rural   ○ apartment   ○ youth

10. Which word has a different number of syllables than the others?
    ○ metal   ○ these   ○ brought

Syllables

For Numbers 1 through 5, read each group of words. Fill in the circle next to the word that is divided correctly into syllables.

1. ○ inter/est   ● for/mu/la   ○ la/un/dr/y

2. ● pres/i/dent   ○ stre/ak   ○ penny

3. ○ sque/eze   ○ de/ve/lo/p   ● a/vail/a/ble

4. ○ reply   ○ ins/ide   ● de/ny

5. ○ ju/dge   ● har/mon/i/ca   ○ suburb/an

For Numbers 6 through 10, read each question. Fill in the circle next to the best answer to each question.

6. Which word has three syllables?
   ● manager   ○ quiet   ○ flipper

7. Which word has the same number of syllables as <u>kangaroo</u>?
   ○ scrape   ○ motion   ● gentleman

8. Which word has two syllables?
   ○ athletic   ● dollar   ○ submarine

9. Which word has the same number of syllables as <u>distant</u>?
   ● rural   ○ apartment   ○ youth

10. Which word has a different number of syllables than the others?
    ● metal   ○ these   ○ brought

Diagnostic Assessment

Sixth Grade
Vocabulary

Vocabulary

The assessments in this section are intended to be completed by a student working independently. The pages for these assessments should be duplicated and distributed to the student. You may find it helpful to read the directions for these assessments out loud before they are administered to ensure that the student understands what to do.

Duplicate the "Student Record" form on page 10 and complete the record for each assessment. You can calculate the percentage correct by hand or look it up in the percentage chart on the inside back cover of this guide. The "Student Record" has space for you to record the observations you make while the student is completing the assessment. Note things such as the speed with which the student works, signs of frustration, attempts at self-correction, and other relevant behaviors.

If some students are having difficulty reading, you may choose to administer the assessments orally. One possibility is to read the assessment to the student and have the student fill in the correct answer. Another possibility is to read the assessment with the student. Allow the student to begin reading, and when the student encounters difficulty, read along with the student until he or she begins reading fluently again.

You may enhance either method of assessment—student reading silently or with your assistance—by asking the student questions like "How do you know that?" or "What makes you sure this answer is right?" The student's answers to these follow-up questions can give you further insight into his or her understanding of the task and his or her ability to read with understanding.

The following chart provides an assessment guideline for each of the sixth-grade Vocabulary assessments.

Assessment	Estimated Percentiles		
	0–49	50–79	80+
Denotation and Connotation (p. 157)	0–3	4–5	6
Compound Words (p. 159)	0–7	8–11	12–15
Multiple-Meaning Words (p. 161)	0–4	5–6	7–8
Word Families (p. 163)	0–5	6–8	9–10
Synonyms and Antonyms (p. 165)	0–5	6–8	9–10
Understanding Idioms (p. 167)	0–4	5–6	7–8
Analogies (p. 169)	0–5	6–8	9–10

Denotation and Connotation

Read each question. Fill in the circle next to the answer you think is correct.

1. In which of these sentences is the denotation of the word *home* closest in meaning to *house?*
   ○ The puppy found a wonderful home with the Langfords.
   ○ The Miller family just bought a new home in our town.
   ○ After years of wandering, Thomas finally felt at home.

2. In which of these sentences is the connotation of *heavy* different in meaning from *weighing a lot?*
   ○ Mark had a heavy heart as he watched his friend leave.
   ○ It took two of us to remove the heavy rock from the garden.
   ○ The heavy blanket kept me warm on the cold night.

3. In which of these sentences is the denotation of the word *good* closest in meaning to *tasty?*
   ○ Everyone believes Mrs. Alberts is a good person.
   ○ Doing good for others is more important than being a success.
   ○ The restaurant wasn't pretty, but the food was good.

4. In which of these sentences is the connotation of *moved* different in meaning from *changed position?*
   ○ The people were moved by the story of the family's rescue.
   ○ The workers moved the house so they could build the road.
   ○ I couldn't see the rabbit in the tall grass until it moved.

5. In which of these sentences is the denotation of the word *free* closest in meaning to *costing nothing?*
   ○ The American colonies wanted to be free from England.
   ○ Tickets to the park were free for students with good grades.
   ○ After months on crutches, Annie was finally free.

6. In which of these sentences is the connotation of *save* different in meaning from *put something away?*
   ○ The money I save will be used for holiday gifts.
   ○ You can save the rest of that sandwich for later.
   ○ Renee's shot helped to save the game for us.

Denotation and Connotation

Read each question. Fill in the circle next to the answer you think is correct.

1. In which of these sentences is the denotation of the word *home* closest in meaning to *house?*
   - ○ The puppy found a wonderful home with the Langfords.
   - ● The Miller family just bought a new home in our town.
   - ○ After years of wandering, Thomas finally felt at home.

2. In which of these sentences is the connotation of *heavy* different in meaning from *weighing a lot?*
   - ● Mark had a heavy heart as he watched his friend leave.
   - ○ It took two of us to remove the heavy rock from the garden.
   - ○ The heavy blanket kept me warm on the cold night.

3. In which of these sentences is the denotation of the word *good* closest in meaning to *tasty?*
   - ○ Everyone believes Mrs. Alberts is a good person.
   - ○ Doing good for others is more important than being a success.
   - ● The restaurant wasn't pretty, but the food was good.

4. In which of these sentences is the connotation of *moved* different in meaning from *changed position?*
   - ● The people were moved by the story of the family's rescue.
   - ○ The workers moved the house so they could build the road.
   - ○ I couldn't see the rabbit in the tall grass until it moved.

5. In which of these sentences is the denotation of the word *free* closest in meaning to *costing nothing?*
   - ○ The American colonies wanted to be free from England.
   - ● Tickets to the park were free for students with good grades.
   - ○ After months on crutches, Annie was finally free.

6. In which of these sentences is the connotation of *save* different in meaning from *put something away?*
   - ○ The money I save will be used for holiday gifts.
   - ○ You can save the rest of that sandwich for later.
   - ● Renee's shot helped to save the game for us.

Diagnostic Assessment

Compound Words

Read each group of words. Fill in the circle next to the compound word in each group.

1. ○ project ○ barnyard ○ wealthy
2. ○ combine ○ release ○ suitcase
3. ○ selected ○ workday ○ blanket
4. ○ classroom ○ employed ○ generation
5. ○ operation ○ attitude ○ yearbook
6. ○ storeroom ○ statement ○ containing
7. ○ establish ○ supported ○ hothouse
8. ○ suggest ○ lakeside ○ instruction
9. ○ bedside ○ territory ○ constantly
10. ○ depending ○ conclusion ○ applesauce
11. ○ silverware ○ smooth ○ edge
12. ○ horizon ○ windshield ○ luxury
13. ○ enormous ○ weary ○ starfish
14. ○ waterfall ○ jumpy ○ notice
15. ○ different ○ miniature ○ paperback

Compound Words

Read each group of words. Fill in the circle next to the compound word in each group.

1. ○ project   ● barnyard   ○ wealthy

2. ○ combine   ○ release   ● suitcase

3. ○ selected   ● workday   ○ blanket

4. ● classroom   ○ employed   ○ generation

5. ○ operation   ○ attitude   ● yearbook

6. ● storeroom   ○ statement   ○ containing

7. ○ establish   ○ supported   ● hothouse

8. ○ suggest   ● lakeside   ○ instruction

9. ● bedside   ○ territory   ○ constantly

10. ○ depending   ○ conclusion   ● applesauce

11. ● silverware   ○ smooth   ○ edge

12. ○ horizon   ● windshield   ○ luxury

13. ○ enormous   ○ weary   ● starfish

14. ● waterfall   ○ jumpy   ○ notice

15. ○ different   ○ miniature   ● paperback

Multiple-Meaning Words

Read each question. Fill in the circle next to the answer you think is correct.

1. In which sentence does the word <u>branch</u> mean "part of a tree"?
   - ○ This <u>branch</u> office opens at ten.
   - ○ The storm last night blew a large <u>branch</u> down.
   - ○ My mother's company will <u>branch</u> out into computer repair.

2. In which sentence does the word <u>race</u> mean "to run fast"?
   - ○ We'll have to <u>race</u> if we want to catch the bus.
   - ○ The governor's <u>race</u> is very close.
   - ○ The human <u>race</u> has adapted to live anywhere on Earth.

3. In which sentence does the word <u>tie</u> mean "an article of clothing"?
   - ○ Help me <u>tie</u> these newspapers together.
   - ○ That <u>tie</u> matches your suit well.
   - ○ The baseball game ended in a <u>tie</u>.

4. In which sentence does the word <u>pole</u> mean "to push a boat"?
   - ○ You will have to <u>pole</u> carefully through the canal.
   - ○ A car backed into the light <u>pole</u> last night.
   - ○ Your fishing <u>pole</u> is in the garage.

5. In which sentence does the word <u>great</u> mean "large"?
   - ○ Evelyn thinks this is a <u>great</u> book.
   - ○ Most people agree that Lincoln was a <u>great</u> president.
   - ○ A <u>great</u> wave crashed over the boat.

6. In which sentence does the word <u>spot</u> mean "see"?
   - ○ This is a great <u>spot</u> for a picnic.
   - ○ Can you <u>spot</u> your sister in the stands?
   - ○ There's a <u>spot</u> on your shirt.

7. In which sentence does the word <u>match</u> mean "a game"?
   - ○ That blue shirt and gray tie are a good <u>match</u>.
   - ○ Use this <u>match</u> to light the candle.
   - ○ The tennis <u>match</u> is almost over.

8. In which sentence does the word <u>part</u> mean "a role in a play"?
   - ○ Carrie will play the <u>part</u> of an astronaut.
   - ○ Which <u>part</u> of the book did you like best?
   - ○ I can never get the <u>part</u> in my hair straight.

Multiple-Meaning Words

Read each question. Fill in the circle next to the answer you think
is correct.

1. In which sentence does the word <u>branch</u> mean "part of a tree"?
   - ○ This <u>branch</u> office opens at ten.
   - ● The storm last night blew a large <u>branch</u> down.
   - ○ My mother's company will <u>branch</u> out into computer repair.

2. In which sentence does the word <u>race</u> mean "to run fast"?
   - ● We'll have to <u>race</u> if we want to catch the bus.
   - ○ The governor's <u>race</u> is very close.
   - ○ The human <u>race</u> has adapted to live anywhere on Earth.

3. In which sentence does the word <u>tie</u> mean "an article of clothing"?
   - ○ Help me <u>tie</u> these newspapers together.
   - ● That <u>tie</u> matches your suit well.
   - ○ The baseball game ended in a <u>tie</u>.

4. In which sentence does the word <u>pole</u> mean "to push a boat"?
   - ● You will have to <u>pole</u> carefully through the canal.
   - ○ A car backed into the light <u>pole</u> last night.
   - ○ Your fishing <u>pole</u> is in the garage.

5. In which sentence does the word <u>great</u> mean "large"?
   - ○ Evelyn thinks this is a <u>great</u> book.
   - ○ Most people agree that Lincoln was a <u>great</u> president.
   - ● A <u>great</u> wave crashed over the boat.

6. In which sentence does the word <u>spot</u> mean "see"?
   - ○ This is a great <u>spot</u> for a picnic.
   - ● Can you <u>spot</u> your sister in the stands?
   - ○ There's a <u>spot</u> on your shirt.

7. In which sentence does the word <u>match</u> mean "a game"?
   - ○ That blue shirt and gray tie are a good <u>match</u>.
   - ○ Use this <u>match</u> to light the candle.
   - ● The tennis <u>match</u> is almost over.

8. In which sentence does the word <u>part</u> mean "a role in a play"?
   - ● Carrie will play the <u>part</u> of an astronaut.
   - ○ Which <u>part</u> of the book did you like best?
   - ○ I can never get the <u>part</u> in my hair straight.

Diagnostic Assessment

Word Families

Read each group of words. Fill in the circle next to the answer that is not in the same word family as the other answers.

1. ○ legislature   ○ legal
   ○ legitimate   ○ lengthen

2. ○ solid   ○ solitary
   ○ solitude   ○ solo

3. ○ beautiful   ○ beautician
   ○ beauty   ○ beaten

4. ○ vital   ○ visualize
   ○ vitamin   ○ vitality

5. ○ touching   ○ tour
   ○ tourist   ○ touring

6. ○ aquarium   ○ aquatic
   ○ aqueduct   ○ acquaint

7. ○ part   ○ partial
   ○ patriot   ○ particle

8. ○ remote   ○ modern
   ○ modernize   ○ modernism

9. ○ region   ○ regular
   ○ regional   ○ regionalize

10. ○ capture   ○ captive
    ○ captain   ○ captivate

Word Families

Read each group of words. Fill in the circle next to the answer that is not in the same word family as the other answers.

1. ○ legislature   ○ legal
   ○ legitimate   ● lengthen

2. ● solid   ○ solitary
   ○ solitude   ○ solo

3. ○ beautiful   ○ beautician
   ○ beauty   ● beaten

4. ○ vital   ● visualize
   ○ vitamin   ○ vitality

5. ● touching   ○ tour
   ○ tourist   ○ touring

6. ○ aquarium   ○ aquatic
   ○ aqueduct   ● acquaint

7. ○ part   ○ partial
   ● patriot   ○ particle

8. ● remote   ○ modern
   ○ modernize   ○ modernism

9. ○ region   ● regular
   ○ regional   ○ regionalize

10. ○ capture   ○ captive
    ● captain   ○ captivate

Synonyms and Antonyms

For Numbers 1 through 5, read each sentence. Fill in the circle next to the synonym for the <u>underlined</u> word in each sentence.

1. Harold hid behind a tree and did not make a <u>sound</u>.
   ○ song   ○ pound   ○ shadow   ○ noise

2. The plane will <u>depart</u> in twenty minutes.
   ○ begin   ○ leave   ○ arrive   ○ disappear

3. Manuel wrote to Hernando, but he received no <u>response</u>.
   ○ mail   ○ question   ○ answer   ○ reason

4. The patient complained that she had headaches <u>frequently</u>.
   ○ often   ○ seldom   ○ never   ○ daily

5. The medical treatments were quite <u>expensive</u>.
   ○ costly   ○ cheap   ○ extensive   ○ relaxing

Read each sentence that follows. Fill in the circle next to the antonym for the <u>underlined</u> word in each sentence.

6. The school rules do not <u>allow</u> radios in the classroom.
   ○ permit   ○ mention   ○ forbid   ○ allot

7. The <u>following</u> announcement is very important.
   ○ next   ○ first   ○ final   ○ preceding

8. The construction workers were <u>building</u> a skyscraper.
   ○ destroying   ○ creating   ○ buying   ○ decorating

9. Finding new energy sources is one of our biggest <u>problems</u>.
   ○ difficulties   ○ solutions   ○ expenses   ○ populations

10. The two <u>enemies</u> finally shook hands and agreed to stop fighting.
    ○ friends   ○ fighters   ○ leaders   ○ soldiers

Synonyms and Antonyms

For Numbers 1 through 5, read each sentence. Fill in the circle next to the synonym for the <u>underlined</u> word in each sentence.

1. Harold hid behind a tree and did not make a <u>sound</u>.
   ○ song   ○ pound   ○ shadow   ● noise

2. The plane will <u>depart</u> in twenty minutes.
   ○ begin   ● leave   ○ arrive   ○ disappear

3. Manuel wrote to Hernando, but he received no <u>response</u>.
   ○ mail   ○ question   ● answer   ○ reason

4. The patient complained that she had headaches <u>frequently</u>.
   ● often   ○ seldom   ○ never   ○ daily

5. The medical treatments were quite <u>expensive</u>.
   ● costly   ○ cheap   ○ extensive   ○ relaxing

Read each sentence that follows. Fill in the circle next to the antonym for the <u>underlined</u> word in each sentence.

6. The school rules do not <u>allow</u> radios in the classroom.
   ○ permit   ○ mention   ● forbid   ○ allot

7. The <u>following</u> announcement is very important.
   ○ next   ○ first   ○ final   ● preceding

8. The construction workers were <u>building</u> a skyscraper.
   ● destroying   ○ creating   ○ buying   ○ decorating

9. Finding new energy sources is one of our biggest <u>problems</u>.
   ○ difficulties   ● solutions   ○ expenses   ○ populations

10. The two <u>enemies</u> finally shook hands and agreed to stop fighting.
    ● friends   ○ fighters   ○ leaders   ○ soldiers

Understanding Idioms

Read each incomplete statement. Fill in the circle next to the answer that best completes each statement.

1. When you "read between the lines," you
   - ○ don't really understand something, but you pretend to.
   - ○ try to figure out if someone is telling the truth or lying.
   - ○ understand the meaning of something beyond the actual words.

2. The expression "you can't have your cake and eat it too" means
   - ○ sometimes you have to decide to take one thing and give up another.
   - ○ if you don't watch what you eat, you will gain too much weight.
   - ○ when you want cake, it's better to eat something else.

3. To "butter someone up" means to
   - ○ embarrass them.
   - ○ flatter them.
   - ○ criticize them.

4. When you "take something with a grain of salt," you
   - ○ are supposed to keep it secret.
   - ○ aren't convinced it's true.
   - ○ don't really want to hear it.

5. If you "give someone the cold shoulder," you
   - ○ ignore them.
   - ○ enjoy them.
   - ○ visit them.

6. Someone who is "all thumbs" is
   - ○ clever.
   - ○ crabby.
   - ○ clumsy.

7. To "get in somebody's hair" means to
   - ○ bother them.
   - ○ understand them.
   - ○ laugh at them.

8. If you "put your foot in your mouth," you
   - ○ say something clever.
   - ○ can't think of anything to say.
   - ○ say something at an inappropriate time.

 167

Name _____ Date _____

Understanding Idioms

Read each incomplete statement. Fill in the circle next to the answer that best completes each statement.

1. When you "read between the lines," you
   - ○ don't really understand something, but you pretend to.
   - ○ try to figure out if someone is telling the truth or lying.
   - ● understand the meaning of something beyond the actual words.

2. The expression "you can't have your cake and eat it too" means
   - ● sometimes you have to decide to take one thing and give up another.
   - ○ if you don't watch what you eat, you will gain too much weight.
   - ○ when you want cake, it's better to eat something else.

3. To "butter someone up" means to
   - ○ embarrass them.
   - ● flatter them.
   - ○ criticize them.

4. When you "take something with a grain of salt," you
   - ○ are supposed to keep it secret.
   - ● aren't convinced it's true.
   - ○ don't really want to hear it.

5. If you "give someone the cold shoulder," you
   - ● ignore them.
   - ○ enjoy them.
   - ○ visit them.

6. Someone who is "all thumbs" is
   - ○ clever.
   - ○ crabby.
   - ● clumsy.

7. To "get in somebody's hair" means to
   - ● bother them.
   - ○ understand them.
   - ○ laugh at them.

8. If you "put your foot in your mouth," you
   - ○ say something clever.
   - ○ can't think of anything to say.
   - ● say something at an inappropriate time.

Diagnostic Assessment

Analogies

Read each analogy. Fill in the circle next to the word that correctly completes the analogy.

1. Stone is to rock as shrub is to _____ .
   ○ flower   ○ bush   ○ vegetable

2. Shoe is to foot as glove is to _____ .
   ○ hand   ○ arm   ○ leg

3. Bread is to food as chair is to _____ .
   ○ room   ○ floor   ○ furniture

4. Clock is to time as thermometer is to _____ .
   ○ size   ○ color   ○ temperature

5. Television is to watch as radio is to _____ .
   ○ listen   ○ taste   ○ touch

6. Tall is to short as heavy is to _____ .
   ○ wide   ○ light   ○ small

7. Street is to city as path is to _____ .
   ○ ocean   ○ animal   ○ forest

8. Slow is to snail as fast is to _____ .
   ○ leaf   ○ rabbit   ○ snow

9. Closet is to clothes as shelf is to _____ .
   ○ tables   ○ pets   ○ books

10. Heat is to fire as light is to _____ .
    ○ stove   ○ lamp   ○ sink

Analogies

Read each analogy. Fill in the circle next to the word that correctly completes the analogy.

1. Stone is to rock as shrub is to _____ .
   ○ flower   ● bush   ○ vegetable

2. Shoe is to foot as glove is to _____ .
   ● hand   ○ arm   ○ leg

3. Bread is to food as chair is to _____ .
   ○ room   ○ floor   ● furniture

4. Clock is to time as thermometer is to _____ .
   ○ size   ○ color   ● temperature

5. Television is to watch as radio is to _____ .
   ● listen   ○ taste   ○ touch

6. Tall is to short as heavy is to _____ .
   ○ wide   ● light   ○ small

7. Street is to city as path is to _____ .
   ○ ocean   ○ animal   ● forest

8. Slow is to snail as fast is to _____ .
   ○ leaf   ● rabbit   ○ snow

9. Closet is to clothes as shelf is to _____ .
   ○ tables   ○ pets   ● books

10. Heat is to fire as light is to _____ .
    ○ stove   ● lamp   ○ sink

Diagnostic Assessment

Silent Reading Comprehension

Silent Reading Comprehension

The assessments in this section are intended to be completed by a student working independently. The pages for these assessments should be duplicated and distributed to the student. You may find it helpful to read the directions for these assessments out loud before they are administered to ensure that the student understands what to do.

Duplicate the "Student Record" form on page 10 and complete the record for each assessment. You can calculate the percentage correct by hand or look it up in the percentage chart on the inside back cover of this guide. The "Student Record" has space for you to record the observations you make while the student is completing the assessment. Note things such as the speed with which the student works, signs of frustration, attempts at self-correction, and other relevant behaviors.

If some students are having difficulty reading, you may choose to administer the assessments orally. One possibility is to read the assessment to the student and have the student fill in the correct answer. Another possibility is to read the assessment with the student. Allow the student to begin reading, and when the student encounters difficulty, read along with the student until he or she begins reading fluently again.

You may enhance either method of assessment—student reading silently or with your assistance—by asking the student questions like "How do you know that?" or "What makes you sure this answer is right?" The student's answers to these follow-up questions can give you further insight into his or her understanding of the task and his or her ability to read with understanding.

The following chart provides an assessment guideline for each of the sixth-grade Silent Reading Comprehension assessments.

Assessment	Estimated Percentiles		
	0–49	50–79	80+
Author's Purpose (p. 173)	0–3	4–5	6
Main Idea and Supporting Details (p. 175)	0–1	2–3	4
Characterization (p. 177)	0–2	3–4	5
Setting (p. 179)	0–1	2–3	4
Sequence (p. 181)	0–1	2–3	4
Drawing Conclusions (p. 183)	0–1	2–3	4

Author's Purpose

Read each paragraph. Fill in the circle next to the reason why the author wrote the paragraph.

1. Mercury is closer to the sun than any other planet. The temperature on the surface of Mercury may be more than 800°F when the sun is shining, but may drop to -300° on the dark side of the planet.
   ○ inform   ○ entertain   ○ convince   ○ explain

2. The spaceship that had left Earth years ago was reaching its destination. Automatic systems began waking the crew, many of whom had been asleep for more than twenty years.
   ○ inform   ○ entertain   ○ convince   ○ explain

3. The railroad station is a comfortable walk from the hotel. As you leave the front door, turn left and walk for three blocks. When you reach Central Avenue, turn right and continue for two blocks. The railroad station is on the left side of the street.
   ○ inform   ○ entertain   ○ convince   ○ explain

4. Washington School needs YOU! This year, we are starting a soccer team, and we hope many of you will come out for the team. You don't need experience. Soccer is an easy game to learn, and several parents have volunteered to coach. If you want to get in on the ground floor, meet at the playground after school.
   ○ inform   ○ entertain   ○ convince   ○ explain

5. Clouds are formed by moisture in Earth's atmosphere. Energy from the sun evaporates water from lakes, streams, and oceans. When this moisture hits cooler air, it condenses into microscopic droplets that form clouds.
   ○ inform   ○ entertain   ○ convince   ○ explain

6. The students who have signed this letter believe our school needs a computer lab that is open at night and on weekends. Many of us don't have computers at home, and we would like to have access to computers outside of normal school hours. It would help us do better in school and prepare for the future.
   ○ inform   ○ entertain   ○ convince   ○ explain

Author's Purpose

Read each paragraph. Fill in the circle next to the reason why the author wrote the paragraph.

1. Mercury is closer to the sun than any other planet. The temperature on the surface of Mercury may be more than 800°F when the sun is shining, but may drop to -300° on the dark side of the planet.
   ● inform   ○ entertain   ○ convince   ○ explain

2. The spaceship that had left Earth years ago was reaching its destination. Automatic systems began waking the crew, many of whom had been asleep for more than twenty years.
   ○ inform   ● entertain   ○ convince   ○ explain

3. The railroad station is a comfortable walk from the hotel. As you leave the front door, turn left and walk for three blocks. When you reach Central Avenue, turn right and continue for two blocks. The railroad station is on the left side of the street.
   ○ inform   ○ entertain   ○ convince   ● explain

4. Washington School needs YOU! This year, we are starting a soccer team, and we hope many of you will come out for the team. You don't need experience. Soccer is an easy game to learn, and several parents have volunteered to coach. If you want to get in on the ground floor, meet at the playground after school.
   ○ inform   ○ entertain   ● convince   ○ explain

5. Clouds are formed by moisture in Earth's atmosphere. Energy from the sun evaporates water from lakes, streams, and oceans. When this moisture hits cooler air, it condenses into microscopic droplets that form clouds.
   ● inform   ○ entertain   ○ convince   ○ explain

6. The students who have signed this letter believe our school needs a computer lab that is open at night and on weekends. Many of us don't have computers at home, and we would like to have access to computers outside of normal school hours. It would help us do better in school and prepare for the future.
   ○ inform   ○ entertain   ● convince   ○ explain

Main Idea and Supporting Details

Read the story and the questions. Fill in the circle next to the best answer to each question.

The lot on the corner of Main and Fourth Streets had been vacant for years. The grocery store that had been there had burned down long ago, and no one had replaced it. The lot had become a dumping ground for trash.

One day, some workers and heavy equipment showed up at the lot. In just one day, they cleared the weeds and trash and began digging a huge hole. No one knew for sure what was going to be built on the corner, but it was clear that it would be huge.

Within a few days, the hole was more than 60 feet deep. Many rumors about the building site were circulating, but no one knew for sure what it would be. Finally, on the fifth day, a sign went up telling what would be built on the corner. It would be a twelve-story, multiuse building with underground parking. The lower eight stories of the building would be a mini-mall, and the upper four stories would be for offices.

Most of the people who lived in the neighborhood were overjoyed. The lot, which was an eyesore, would be replaced with an attractive building. In addition, the new stores would offer jobs and recreation opportunities. A few people griped about the traffic the new mini-mall would bring, but the vast majority of the people in the neighborhood thought it was a great development.

1. What is the main idea of this story?
   ○ Most of the people in a neighborhood support a mini-mall.
   ○ A mysterious building is being constructed in a city.
   ○ A vacant lot is being converted to a new mini-mall.

2. What is the purpose of the deep hole?
   ○ underground parking
   ○ office space
   ○ stores and restaurants

3. Why did rumors start about the building?
   ○ People in the neighborhood were suspicious.
   ○ No one knew for certain what it would be.
   ○ The builder wanted it to be a surprise.

4. What is a potential disadvantage of the mini-mall?
   ○ It may cause traffic to get worse.
   ○ It may provide jobs for people.

 175

Main Idea and Supporting Details

Read the story and the questions. Fill in the circle next to the best answer to each question.

The lot on the corner of Main and Fourth Streets had been vacant for years. The grocery store that had been there had burned down long ago, and no one had replaced it. The lot had become a dumping ground for trash.

One day, some workers and heavy equipment showed up at the lot. In just one day, they cleared the weeds and trash and began digging a huge hole. No one knew for sure what was going to be built on the corner, but it was clear that it would be huge.

Within a few days, the hole was more than 60 feet deep. Many rumors about the building site were circulating, but no one knew for sure what it would be. Finally, on the fifth day, a sign went up telling what would be built on the corner. It would be a twelve-story, multiuse building with underground parking. The lower eight stories of the building would be a mini-mall, and the upper four stories would be for offices.

Most of the people who lived in the neighborhood were overjoyed. The lot, which was an eyesore, would be replaced with an attractive building. In addition, the new stores would offer jobs and recreation opportunities. A few people griped about the traffic the new mini-mall would bring, but the vast majority of the people in the neighborhood thought it was a great development.

1. What is the main idea of this story?
   - ○ Most of the people in a neighborhood support a mini-mall.
   - ○ A mysterious building is being constructed in a city.
   - ● A vacant lot is being converted to a new mini-mall.

2. What is the purpose of the deep hole?
   - ● underground parking
   - ○ office space
   - ○ stores and restaurants

3. Why did rumors start about the building?
   - ○ People in the neighborhood were suspicious.
   - ● No one knew for certain what it would be.
   - ○ The builder wanted it to be a surprise.

4. What is a potential disadvantage of the mini-mall?
   - ● It may cause traffic to get worse.
   - ○ It may provide jobs for people.

Characterization

Read the story and the questions. Fill in the circle next to the best answer to each question.

Harrison Fillmore III was lazy and selfish. Never in his entire life had Harrison made his own bed, hung up his own clothes, or put away his own books and papers. When others didn't do something for him, he pouted and sulked in his room. That's why he was shocked by his cousin Rudy's behavior when Rudy came to visit. The first thing Rudy did (after carrying his own bag to his room) was unpack the bag without any help.

"We have servants to do those things for us," Harrison smirked.

"Why?" Rudy asked. "Don't you know how to do them?"

Rudy made his own bed every morning and straightened up his room before he had breakfast.

Harrison's mother blamed Rudy's strange behavior on her sister, Rudy's mother.

"Cecily is a little odd," Mrs. Fillmore said to her husband. "Why, she even works somewhere in the city doing something."

"She's an accountant," Mr. Fillmore answered, "and a good one. I think she's doing a fine job with Rudy. Young Harrison could learn a thing or two from his cousin."

"Don't be silly," Mrs. Fillmore said. "Harrison is fine just the way he is."

1. The author shows that Harrison is _____ .
   ○ boring   ○ spoiled   ○ careful

2. The author shows that Rudy is _____ .
   ○ spoiled   ○ foolish   ○ self-reliant

3. The author shows that Mrs. Fillmore is _____ .
   ○ strange   ○ jealous   ○ snobbish

4. Mrs. Fillmore's words show that she _____ .
   ○ disapproves of Rudy   ○ likes Rudy   ○ admires her sister

5. Mr. Fillmore's words show that he _____ .
   ○ approves of Rudy   ○ disapproves of Cecily   ○ approves of Harrison

Characterization

Read the story and the questions. Fill in the circle next to the best
answer to each question.

Harrison Fillmore III was lazy and selfish. Never in his entire life
had Harrison made his own bed, hung up his own clothes, or put away
his own books and papers. When others didn't do something for him, he
pouted and sulked in his room. That's why he was shocked by his cousin
Rudy's behavior when Rudy came to visit. The first thing Rudy did (after
carrying his own bag to his room) was unpack the bag without any help.

"We have servants to do those things for us," Harrison smirked.

"Why?" Rudy asked. "Don't you know how to do them?"

Rudy made his own bed every morning and straightened up his
room before he had breakfast.

Harrison's mother blamed Rudy's strange behavior on her sister,
Rudy's mother.

"Cecily is a little odd," Mrs. Fillmore said to her husband. "Why, she
even works somewhere in the city doing something."

"She's an accountant," Mr. Fillmore answered, "and a good one. I
think she's doing a fine job with Rudy. Young Harrison could learn a
thing or two from his cousin."

"Don't be silly," Mrs. Fillmore said. "Harrison is fine just the way he is."

1. The author shows that Harrison is _____ .
   ○ boring ● spoiled ○ careful

2. The author shows that Rudy is _____ .
   ○ spoiled ○ foolish ● self-reliant

3. The author shows that Mrs. Fillmore is _____ .
   ○ strange ○ jealous ● snobbish

4. Mrs. Fillmore's words show that she _____ .
   ● disapproves of Rudy ○ likes Rudy ○ admires her sister

5. Mr. Fillmore's words show that he _____ .
   ● approves of Rudy ○ disapproves of Cecily ○ approves of Harrison

Setting

Read the sentence. Fill in the circle next to the phrase that correctly completes the sentence.

1. The setting of the story includes _____ .
   ○ the order of events in the story
   ○ the location and time in which the events take place
   ○ the most important series of events
   ○ the descriptions of the characters

Read the passages. Fill in the circle next to the correct answer to each question.

A. Ali woke up and stretched lazily. It was still early, and the crisp fall air felt good on his face. He could hardly believe he was here. For more than a month he had been looking forward to camping in the mountains of Nevada.

B. Four, three, two, one, zero! Well, we're off, and it's time to stop trying to think what else we might need during our fifteen months on Mars. Anything forgotten will have to wait until next year.

C. It is October 28, 1886. Just a few hours ago, here on Bedloe's Island in New York Harbor, thousands of people watched as France's gift to the United States was unveiled. I am so proud to be one of the first people to see this great Statue of Liberty.

D. Kyoko was grateful that she was not alone when the elevator got stuck on her way up from lunch. Still, the smells of perfume and ripe fruit mingling with her lunch were far from appetizing. She hoped she would not have to share this warm, dimly lit space for long. Even the air conditioner had stopped.

2. Which passage has the smallest setting?
   ○ A   ○ B   ○ C   ○ D

3. Which passages indicate the time of year?
   ○ A and B   ○ A and C   ○ B and C   ○ B and D

4. Which passage takes place in the future?
   ○ A   ○ B   ○ C   ○ D

Setting

Read the sentence. Fill in the circle next to the phrase that correctly completes the sentence.

1. The setting of the story includes _____ .
   - ○ the order of events in the story
   - ● the location and time in which the events take place
   - ○ the most important series of events
   - ○ the descriptions of the characters

Read the passages. Fill in the circle next to the correct answer to each question.

A. Ali woke up and stretched lazily. It was still early, and the crisp fall air felt good on his face. He could hardly believe he was here. For more than a month he had been looking forward to camping in the mountains of Nevada.

B. Four, three, two, one, zero! Well, we're off, and it's time to stop trying to think what else we might need during our fifteen months on Mars. Anything forgotten will have to wait until next year.

C. It is October 28, 1886. Just a few hours ago, here on Bedloe's Island in New York Harbor, thousands of people watched as France's gift to the United States was unveiled. I am so proud to be one of the first people to see this great Statue of Liberty.

D. Kyoko was grateful that she was not alone when the elevator got stuck on her way up from lunch. Still, the smells of perfume and ripe fruit mingling with her lunch were far from appetizing. She hoped she would not have to share this warm, dimly lit space for long. Even the air conditioner had stopped.

2. Which passage has the smallest setting?
   ○ A   ○ B   ○ C   ● D

3. Which passages indicate the time of year?
   ○ A and B   ● A and C   ○ B and C   ○ B and D

4. Which passage takes place in the future?
   ○ A   ● B   ○ C   ○ D

Diagnostic Assessment

Sequence

Read the passage and the sentences. Fill in the circle next to the phrase that correctly completes the sentence.

To become a law, a bill introduced in the United States House of Representatives must go through several steps. First, the bill is sent to a committee of the House. If a bill is very important, the committee may hold public hearings so that people for and against the bill can speak. When the hearings are over, the committee votes on whether or not to send the bill to the whole House for approval or rejection. If it is sent to the whole House, a bill can go through a long period of debate and amendment. Then, if the House votes to approve it, the House version of the bill is sent to the Senate, which goes through a similar procedure to produce its own version. After this, differences in the Senate and House versions of the bill have to be worked out by both bodies. The final version of the bill is sent to the president of the United States. If the president signs the bill, it becomes a law.

1. Before it goes to the whole House for approval or rejection, a bill must first be _____ .
   ○ sent to the Senate
   ○ sent to a House committee
   ○ sent to the president

2. If a bill is sent to the whole House of Representatives, it can be _____ .
   ○ debated and amended
   ○ signed by the president
   ○ approved by the Senate

3. After the House approves its version of the bill, the bill is _____ .
   ○ sent to the president
   ○ debated and amended
   ○ sent to the Senate

4. After the House and Senate work out a final version of the bill, it is _____ .
   ○ sent to a committee
   ○ sent to the president
   ○ debated and amended

Diagnostic Assessment **181**

Sequence

Read the passage and the sentences. Fill in the circle next to the phrase that correctly completes the sentence.

To become a law, a bill introduced in the United States House of Representatives must go through several steps. First, the bill is sent to a committee of the House. If a bill is very important, the committee may hold public hearings so that people for and against the bill can speak. When the hearings are over, the committee votes on whether or not to send the bill to the whole House for approval or rejection. If it is sent to the whole House, a bill can go through a long period of debate and amendment. Then, if the House votes to approve it, the House version of the bill is sent to the Senate, which goes through a similar procedure to produce its own version. After this, differences in the Senate and House versions of the bill have to be worked out by both bodies. The final version of the bill is sent to the president of the United States. If the president signs the bill, it becomes a law.

1. Before it goes to the whole House for approval or rejection, a bill must first be _____ .
   ○ sent to the Senate
   ● sent to a House committee
   ○ sent to the president

2. If a bill is sent to the whole House of Representatives, it can be _____ .
   ● debated and amended
   ○ signed by the president
   ○ approved by the Senate

3. After the House approves its version of the bill, the bill is _____ .
   ○ sent to the president
   ○ debated and amended
   ● sent to the Senate

4. After the House and Senate work out a final version of the bill, it is _____ .
   ○ sent to a committee
   ● sent to the president
   ○ debated and amended

Drawing Conclusions

Read the story and the questions. Fill in the circle next to the best answer to each question.

The new mall had been under construction for two years. Now that it was almost ready to open, the students at the Poplar Avenue School were in for a surprise. The management of the mall was planning a special day before the opening for students, teachers, and their families. They would have the whole mall to themselves, and all the stores would be open and ready for business.

The school was just a few blocks from the mall, and when it had been proposed, many people were concerned. Parents and others thought mall traffic might pose a hazard to students going to school. They were also worried that students might find going to the mall more interesting than going to school. The owners of the mall had met with parents and had responded to all their concerns. They had even established a branch library in the mall that included a computer lab.

1. The special day for students, teachers, and their families is probably
   ○ a way to make a lot of money before the official opening of the mall.
   ○ an effort to show that the mall can be a good neighbor to the school.
   ○ a good way to see if traffic from the mall will affect the school.

2. Which of these is a traffic problem the mall might create?
   ○ Cars coming to the mall will be dangerous for students walking or riding the bus.
   ○ At night, drivers would have a difficult time seeing students going to school.
   ○ The mall parking lot would be so crowded that parents, teachers, and buses would have no place to park.

3. What is the meaning of the phrase "students might find going to the mall more interesting than going to school"?
   ○ Students would learn more at the mall than in school.
   ○ Students might get into trouble at the mall.
   ○ Students might skip school and go to the mall.

4. How will the special day for students, teachers, and their families help the people who work at the mall?
   ○ It will make them learn the fastest way to get to the mall.
   ○ It will serve as a kind of practice without huge crowds.
   ○ It will help them decide if the school is where their children should go.

Diagnostic Assessment **183**

Drawing Conclusions

Read the story and the questions. Fill in the circle next to the best answer to each question.

The new mall had been under construction for two years. Now that it was almost ready to open, the students at the Poplar Avenue School were in for a surprise. The management of the mall was planning a special day before the opening for students, teachers, and their families. They would have the whole mall to themselves, and all the stores would be open and ready for business.

The school was just a few blocks from the mall, and when it had been proposed, many people were concerned. Parents and others thought mall traffic might pose a hazard to students going to school. They were also worried that students might find going to the mall more interesting than going to school. The owners of the mall had met with parents and had responded to all their concerns. They had even established a branch library in the mall that included a computer lab.

1. The special day for students, teachers, and their families is probably
   ○ a way to make a lot of money before the official opening of the mall.
   ● an effort to show that the mall can be a good neighbor to the school.
   ○ a good way to see if traffic from the mall will affect the school.

2. Which of these is a traffic problem the mall might create?
   ● Cars coming to the mall will be dangerous for students walking or riding the bus.
   ○ At night, drivers would have a difficult time seeing students going to school.
   ○ The mall parking lot would be so crowded that parents, teachers, and buses would have no place to park.

3. What is the meaning of the phrase "students might find going to the mall more interesting than going to school"?
   ○ Students would learn more at the mall than in school.
   ○ Students might get into trouble at the mall.
   ● Students might skip school and go to the mall.

4. How will the special day for students, teachers, and their families help the people who work at the mall?
   ○ It will make them learn the fastest way to get to the mall.
   ● It will serve as a kind of practice without huge crowds.
   ○ It will help them decide if the school is where their children should go.